MW00902391

ISBN-13: 978-1514192979

ISBN-10: 1514192977

PUBLISHED BY: AMB/FAM CARTEL PRODUCTIONS

COVER ART: AMB PUBLISHING PRODUCTIONS

COVER MODEL: PRINCESS AMIRA

PHOTOGRAPHER: ROLAND HATCH

EDIT: KENYA BAKER

To order additional copies of this book, contact:

Shaunta Kenerly

Follow me on Twitter @shaunkenerly

shauntakenerly@yahoo.com

follow the book & myself on facebook

ESCAPING THE ALLURE OF THE GAME

Shaunta M. Kenerly

DEDICATION

This book is dedicated to my children. I thank God for putting you all in my life, to keep me motivated to do right and be a father to you all. I love you all and I will continue to show you every day that I am blessed to be on this earth. Thank you.

ACKNOWLEDGEMENTS

I give thanks to God for blessing me with this gift. He placed me in a position for years so that I could clear my mind and realize what is important to me in life. I thank Him for giving me a creative mind to write these stories written while I was incarcerated. It is not the amount of time but what you do with it.

I would like to thank my mother, Lora Kenerly, for being a strong, loving, kind, wonderful soul. She did her best raising the three of us, and I am blessed for you to be my mother. I will not trade you for anything.

My list of acknowledgments can go a long way but I must say my sister Melissa stayed on me to write and enjoyed each piece of the book I had mailed to her. My boy Fred, thank you my friend, my brother Chris for your support and keeping me positive. Thanks to all my supporters in Louisville, KY, Mount Sterling, KY, Madison Correctional whom I was incarcerated with that showed me love. I will not forget any of y'all. Thanks to my Dayton city streets for giving me the mind, the attitude, and teaching me all that I need to know about the game. I am turning a negative to a positive.

CHAPTER 1

REESE

Tonight the crew and I rode four deep on interstate 75 heading south to Cincinnati in a heavy rainstorm. We all loaded up to meet with our new connect, some Haitians who have been pushing some major weight down here for years.

My crew was made up of myself, but I go by Reese for short, Maurice my two best friends B and Tone, and my wild young gun White Boy. In fact, White Boy is the reason why we're in this position in the first place.

Our last connect we did business with for years and we all made a good living over the time. About two months ago, business begun to take a down slide because the coke wasn't consistently good to move. The whole crew felt the effects in our banking accounts. I remained humble not getting upset about our loss in financial gain unlike White Boy. We continued to make moves with what we had, while waiting for things to turn around.

Each time we would take the trip to New York or meet up with Big Mike at our drop spot, White Boy tried to come up with some scheme to stick Big Mike up or protested why we should stop doing business with the crooked ass nigga. I would just ignore White Boy's ass and sometimes laughed at some of his idea, but deep down we all understood where he was coming from.

White Boy constantly told us Big Mike was selling us the bad work purposely but would give us a good batch from time to time to prevent us from finding a new connect. He made some valid points but I had to put food on the table. He wanted us to buy our weight from some Hispanics who hustled on the other side of the city. Not wanting to take the chance on taking a loss or creating any more problems, we decided against it and remained loyal customers to Big Mike until last week.

Big Mike and his team met us at our usual drop spot, an abandoned warehouse to sell us five bricks of coke he claimed he had left over from making a drop in Detroit. The call could not have come at a better time for us as we were low on dope and needed some more work to last us the rest of the month, so we grabbed the cash and weapons for protection and we were in route to the meeting spot. Normally, B and I would do all of the business work and socializing while Tone and White Boy watched our backs. This time White Boy insisted on handling business alone while we stood guard. B and Tone stood watching Big Mike's men as I kept my eyes on White Boy. Before I realized the scenario, White Boy had his .45 pistol aimed at Big Mike's chest and we didn't hesitate to pull our guns out, catching his men off guard. After a heated trade of threats, White Boy snatched the dope and we peeled out, leaving their faces in the cloud of dirt.

I was upset with White Boy choosing the wrong time to pull off this scheme from Big Mike, only getting five bricks, when we could have waited and got a lot more. What had me even more upset was that the five bricks only lasted us a couple days and we hadn't had any work since, In this game, a day is too long to go without work and could result in losing a lot of money and respect from the streets.

During our drought, our cell phones have been ringing off the hook like phone sex lines on a late night. The city of Dayton streets were starving for work and we needed to feed it before another crew brings dinner. I'm desperate to get another connect who would be able to get us together but it has to be a strong connect. White Boy tried again to persuade me to buy from the Hispanics but I decided against it because I had to know the people we were dealing with. We could not afford to make war in the streets at this time.

The only person I knew with ties to some major weight was an old school hustler named Keith. I called and asked him for help. We all looked up to Keith because he was a street legend. In Keith's hustling days, he was always a step ahead of the game having the police in his pockets and hoods backing him with protection. He had his reign in the early nineties holding the whole city of Dayton down, as well as other cities within Ohio. He was a star within his own state and even attracted wannabe kingpins and hip hop stars here. He used them to build on his name adding more power to his empire. After Keith's older brother Kevin aka, Cash, was murdered during a drug deal, Keith decided to give it all up and leave the game alone while he was still breathing. He chose another direction with his life, but never gave up his hustling spirit, smartly investing his money with legitimate businesses. What we all respected most about Keith is that no matter what the situation was, he would look out for us. He always tried to instill in me to show love to everyone and I would get that in return. Keith molded me from a corner nigga who sold pieces to the nigga buying bricks today. He told all about his mistakes and lessons, in order to keep me from an early grave like his brother. Keith taught me everything I knew about hustling and I took each lesson as a blessing keeping me alive and paid. Although Keith retired from the game, he knows everything and every major nigga pushing weight around the state. When I told him about what happened between us and Big Mike he didn't hesitate to hook us up with our new Haitian connect.

So now we're in Tone's new Suburban and I'm in the passenger seat watching the windshield wipers rapidly swish away the pouring raindrops. Over the sound of the windshield wipers and speakers blasting some local artist, I overhear B and White Boy arguing from the backseat. I'm trying to tune in on the disagreement but my cell phone vibrates on my belt clip. I check my caller ID and to my surprise its Keith calling.

"What's up boy? Y'all get right yet?" Keith asked.

"We're riding up the street now. Everything is all right over there, right?" I replied.

"Yes! I just thought y'all would have been there and finished business by now. Don't worry about anything my boy, James is all about business. Reese, y'all just have that money and he'll get y'all all the way together."

"Oh, we have the money ready. I just want to be in and out hitting the highway as soon as possible," I replied

"Well as soon as y'all get done don't forget to come by the club. You know tonight I'm having the opening for the strip club?" Keith asked.

After a brief pause I spoke, "Damn, I almost forgot! Soon as we drop the work off we'll be on our way."

"I'll have the ladies waiting for y'all to show," Keith chuckled.

"We'll make sure that your ladies have a good night."

"I have some real video vixens working in here. Tell those niggas that it is going down and not to spend all of their money all in one spot," Keith chuckles again. "Well Reese, let me get this place together and make sure these women are ready to make love to this money."

"A'ight, look for us to be there between 10:30 and 11 o'clock."

"Y'all be safe," Keith said ending the call.

Suddenly, B shouts, "What the fuck are you looking for?"

White Boy shot back a mean mug at B. "My .45! B you have to be ready for anything at any moment."

"Nigga I got mine right here," B said patting his pistol on his shoulder holster. "You're acting as if you're getting ready to go to war. If Keith and Cash fucked with these muthafuckas then there isn't much to worry about."

"You act like you know these muthafuckas personally or have bought some shit from them before. I do not know these muthafuckas and

I do not trust these muthafuckas. I do know that if these niggas catch you slipping just a little you won't get a second chance to get them back," White Boy responded by pulling out the gun from under his seat.

Tone sat up from his lean in the seat and turned the stereo off. "We're about to pull up on the house. White Boy, calm the fuck down and get ready for these muthafuckas. Don't be on your bullshit because you'll get a lot of people killed.

I turned around in my seat so I can look directly at White Boy. "Look bruh we need these muthafuckas all right? We're businessmen and so are they. They want to get paid just as we do. We can't afford for anything to jump off. These are Keith's people and two hundred stacks are too much to take a loss on.

White Boys eyes widened. "Bro we're not going to take a loss, believe that.

"I see what Reese is saying and White Boy I feel you also. Let us just go in here handle business and get this work safely back home," B added.

"Right," Tone interjected.

"Far as if anything pops off it is what it is," B said.

"Um, White Boy do me a favor," I wait for a response.

"What up?"

"While B and I are talking to James, I want you to watch our backs."

"Don't I always? You don't have to worry about a thing man, I got y'all," White Boy said.

I'd let out a loud laugh. "Just don't get trigger happy man."

Tone pointed out the windshield. "This is the address for the house. Reese while y'all talking business I'll hold on to the money."

"That's what up."

"White Boy are you ready?" B questioned clinching onto the door handle.

"You know I am!" White Boy shouted.

Soon as Tone turned off the headlights, someone approaches the door. I reached over to tap Tone but he's already nodding to let me know he sees what I see. B tossed the duffel bags of money to Tone, and then we exit the truck and walk to the front door. I'd studied White Boy's body language making sure he isn't on anything tonight. I couldn't predict what he's thinking or wanted to do so I silently asked God to look over us.

At the door stood this tall muscle bound muthafucka. His dark complexion and long dreads assured me that we're at the right house. He wore his dreads tied back and showed off his physique wearing a tight black tank top. Resting on top of his left shoulder was a double-barrel shotgun. B and I stood at the entrance and I noticed the man towers over me and I'm 6'2". He looked like he should play pro football.

While he tried to intimidate somebody with his dead stare, a bad ass bitch walked up. Her face is beautiful with her rich chocolate skin. I loved her piercing above her lip; it complemented her dimples when she talked.

"Open the bag so I can take a look inside." She instructed Tone with her island accent.

Tone halfway unzipped the bags allowing her to get just a peek and slide her arm inside checking for any weapons. Then she looked directly at me and orders me to raise my arms. I laughed quietly and gradually lift my arms. She stepped in front of me and began her search all over my body. Instantly she found my pistol on my waist but continued to conduct her thorough search. Kneeling down, she rubbed her hands between my thighs moving her hands slowly up. I'd looked down patiently, waiting for her to move up a few more inches. We locked eyes for a split second, and then she intentionally grabs my dick firmly, blushing hard enough for me to see her deep dimples. Bad as I wanted her to pull it out and stick it in her mouth, she side steps me and stands in front of White Boy. Before she can instruct him to do anything, he informed her that she can stop at him because we all have weapons on us.

She screwed up her face, then turned away yelling toward the back of the house, "J they're here and they all have guns on them!"

"Why shouldn't they have guns on them?" A voice emerges from the back. "Just bring them on back and bring the shit," J ordered in a strong island accent.

Walking down the hallway, I'd glanced over my shoulder and notice White Boy behind me gripping his pistol hard as hell. This nigga be tripping I think to myself. I gave him a look that said to calm the fuck down. He was giving off an angry kind of energy due to the big guy walking right behind him step by step. We reached the end of the hallway and four more Haitian men sit in positions with automatic weapons. All of them have their fingers inches away from the trigger.

J sat on a blood red leather sofa smoking on some high-grade weed. Keith had described J to me before we had come down. Focused on his chess match, he doesn't look up at us. J's men kept their eyes on him and rotate them back on us. Their demeanor shows me that J was more than respected, he is feared. On the wall behind J hung a huge flag of Haiti.

The girl who led us to him reminded him of our presence. J made his next move before turning to us.

"Welcome brothers," He blows out a cloud of smoke. "Bring the dope now woman," J instructed the girl, waving his sparkling diamond bracelet for her to leave.

"I'm glad that you are giving us this opportunity to make this money with you." I shook his hand firmly, noticing his rings on his hands. J took another hit from the blunt before speaking, "You are Keith's boys? He told me nothing but good news about all of you. Most importantly, he said you boys can get rid of a lot of weight."

"Yeah we go through a lot, but we have the ability to sell more if we can get a solid connect close to home," B responded.

"Which of you boys are B and Reese…?" J questioned eye balling all of us.

"That's us," I said pointing at B and myself.

"Keith spoke more about you two than the others, so no disrespect to your boys but I'm only discussing business with you two."

"Nah, that's all right. B, we'll stand right over there," Tone said.

J placed the blunt down in the ashtray. "You boys take a seat. Either of you know how to play chess?"

B smirked since we battle at chess whenever one of us decides to talk shit. "Yeah, we go at it from time to time."

Chess is a man's mind game. You can learn a lot about your opponent from the way he moves his chess pieces." J speaks like a college professor. "Let's get down to business and you boys tell me how much weight can you handle?"

"Now no disrespect to you but Keith must have misled you. We're here to buy our own. We appreciate the offer but we can buy our own," I interject.

J's men eyes widened and one stands to his feet preparing himself. He just needs J to give him the word and he'll be shooting.

J waved the guard off. "I like your style. Now I see why Keith speaks so highly of you."

"We'll take ten bricks off your hands if it's the way Keith tells us," B casually said.

"I have ten for you boys and more. Trust me, there isn't any dope out here like I have."

"We normally pay eighteen five a piece. Keith said that it shouldn't be a problem matching the price," I said.

"Look, this is what I can do for you boys," J responds picking his blunt back up. "Since you boys fuck with my boy Keith, I will let the dope go for twenty apiece. But listen here, you boys keep fucking with me and I'll lower the price to seventeen five."

We can definitely do that. Twenty isn't bad and we can't wait to get the other deal," I said with excitement.

"Tone, let me get the money," B grabs the bags then hands them over to J.

"You boys already had in mind the amount I would say and it's ready for me," J said peeking inside the bag on his lap.

"It's all there, there's no need to count," B interjected while J continued to look inside.

"I believe you but I still have to check. So you knew that I would ask for twenty a piece?"

"No but we knew that you're a man of business and would give us a fair offer. You're a business man and so are we," B replied.

J smiled and snicker. After hitting his blunt and exhaling, he passed the bags to the person he was playing chess with.

The girl re-entered the room with another guard and they're both holding duffel bags. I got a sense of nervousness reminiscing on the last time we were trying to buy some weight and White Boy laid them down. I looked over at B and he seems normal. Then I turned to look for White Boy and Tone and their faces seem focused and ready for anything to happen. I become calm and reminded myself that this is another situation with someone who isn't set to get one over on us.

J sent the girl a nod allowing her to conduct the trade.

"Do you want to hold the other bag?" She asked me in a soft voice.

"I'll take the bags lil' momma," Tone interjected.

"Do you boys want to test the product?" J asked.

"No, we're good. We know where we can find you," Tone replied.

"I like you boys more and more. You boys have a lot of heart I have to say that," J laughed.

"We'll be ready for more soon. Will you have some ready for us then?" I asked.

"I'm always ready. You boys keep doing business with me and I will make sure you will be set for life like our friend Keith. You give me a call whenever you need some more and we'll do business again."

"All right we'll do that. We'll definitely be seeing you again and I have your number locked in my phone," I replied.

Once again, the big nigga and the fine ass island girl follow us through the house. Now we're heading home with ten bricks, ready to put the work on the streets.

CHAPTER 2

REESE

The rain stopped and everyone's focus is getting home safe. The interstate is known to have state troopers just waiting for a bust. We all sat quietly and alert watching for anything out of the ordinary. Tone hid the bags of dope under some laundry. White Boy also hid B's and my guns in a compartment under his seat. Tone put his pistol in his glove compartment and stored his clips on the side of his door. Everything was set into play, but I'll not feel comfortable until I reach the city lines.

Seeing the downtown skyline, I felt at ease. Being back in familiar surroundings made things right. Looking over at the stereo, I notice that it is 10:30, and remember I told Keith we'd stop by his club tonight. I have to go and support him by showing his women love so I pull out my cell to call Keith and see I've missed several calls. Most are from my girl Diana. I had my phone on silent so it wouldn't alarm anybody. She's probably a nervous wreck.

I click on her name. "Hi baby are you still up?"

"Now you decide to call." I can hear her smacking her lips.

"Diana you know what I'm out here doing, so please don't start that bullshit."

"I don't have anything to say to you Reese,"

"Just answer this for me—"

"What boy?" she says irritated.

"Can you stay up a while longer for me?" I beg. Not too much longer Reese. I'm tired. I'm already in the bed. I've been waiting on you to come home for hours now. I had something special planned for you tonight but you want to take your time."

As soon as the words rolled off her tongue I knew what she meant. She was going to let me in on one of her Vicky secrets.

"Baby I'll be home in a few hours. We just hopped on the highway not too long ago," I lied to spare some time.

"I'm tired from work and all I wanted was you tonight. I've been trying to call you for the past hour and you couldn't answer. You tell me what that is about Reese."

"Diana—" I utter but I'm cut off again.

"You can't keep doing me like this," she whines.

"I know babe. Soon as we're done handling business, I'm coming straight home to you. Trust me baby, it won't be much longer." I pleaded with her.

"Well I'm going to take a hot shower and prepare myself for you," she says in a soft voice.

"Yeah baby, please do that for me."

"You know I know how to treat my man."

"Yes you do. I'll be there as soon as I can…" The chime informing that someone is calling interrupts me. I check the caller ID. It's Keith. "Babe Keith is calling; I need to answer this. Can you hold on for just a second so I can find out what he wants?"

"No Reese! I don't want you to end up out all night."

"Baby just hold on, damn! This will only take a second," I reply aggressively hearing the phone chime again.

"Whatever," she says sternly.

"I love you, now let me answer this." I say to click over without waiting for a response...

"What up?" I spat.

"Shit what up? You sound pissed off," Keith said.

"Man, wifey as usual. She doesn't understand that I have to put in work so that we can continue to live well and have the life she wants."

"They never do, until times get hard. You just have to learn how to be Reese and Maurice. Take care of home then take care of business."

"Right..."

"The money is about to start flowing in and things will get better for y'all. This is big business for you. Keep your team tight and there won't be any limits on what y'all will become. Y'all will only be as strong as y'all weakest link," Keith philosophizes.

"I know," I replied allowing his words to sink in.

"Now that's said, how did everything go down there?"

"Everything went good. The James nigga is feeling us already."

"He took care of y'all huh? That's my boy. J is a good nigga, he'll look out for a muthafucka who is trying to get it."

"We'll be doing more business with him. Shit, I'm glad we have a solid connect now who we can count on to put us on at any time."

"I love them Natti niggas and they and will take care of y'all if y'all play your cards right. Stay on top of the game Reese."

I heard the music in the background of the club grow louder and figure he's walking throughout the club. "Keith I can barely hear you now!" I tried to talk over the music.

"You know that I have to have the music hitting for the ladies!" Keith shouted.

"Keith, wifey is still on the other end but we'll be there as soon we drop off the work."

"Handle your business, I'll see y'all later."

"A'ight." I ended the call.

Clicking back over the line is dead. She's mad at me for leaving her on hold for so long. It's necessary that I call her as soon as we finish with everything. I placed the phone in my pocket and my mind begins to race with thoughts about her.

"Reese was that Keith?" B asked.

"Yeah…, I told him that everything was good. He wants us to come by his new strip club tonight."

"Oh yeah, we're there!" White Boy shouted.

"Keith is going to have that muthafucka jumping. I know that he has some bad ass bitches going hard in there," Tone said.

"Let's drop this work off and then we can shoot right over there. We have a few stacks at the house we can use to show out for tonight. Amad should be there with the money he made now. Matter of fact, let me call him now." B said pulling out his cell phone.

Amad was a childhood friend of ours but he left the hood for a few years to go to college only to come back. He was kicked out of school after he got caught selling some weed from his dorm room. Not being able to find a job, he asked to work for us. We allow him to sell dope by the ounces getting the grind money. Amad gathered up a young crew of hustlers to get rid of most of the work for him on the streets. His crew helps us get rid of the work a lot faster and the money is always right.

"What up man, are you at the house?" B questioned after putting us on speakerphone.

"Yeah I'm here. When are y'all coming through so I can get back to the money? My phone has been ringing off the hook," Amad stressed.

"We'll be there in a few minutes. Do you have the money ready?" B asked.

"Yeah I have the money bruh! I'm just waiting on y'all!" Amad exclaimed.

"Yeah okay...,"

"B, I want to talk to you and the team about some other business. I have some college friends that need to get down with us. They ran into a problem like we had with their connect and now need some work fast. They can get rid of the shit as soon as they can get their hands on it and be back to buy more. We should really think about expanding our business and fuck with these niggas while we can."

"Open the damn door then nigga. We've been out here just checking to see if you are on your toes. Anybody could have run up on your ass. There is no room for error bruh. Get focused." B instructed.

"Shit, I'm just watching this freak movie and blowing some loud kush. I'm focused B, trust me."

"Yeah whatever, come open the door."

The house where we kept our dope is in the hood we all grew up in. We remained to keep ties to our hood and all the neighbors know us well. Most importantly, everyone knows we're Keith's boys so we're not the ones to be fucked with. We didn't have to worry about any neighbors calling the police because we do little things in the community for the kids. We also keep a low profile. Amad's crew was the only traffic coming to the house. White Boy oversees all operation here watching Amad closely making sure shit is ran smoothly. White Boy and Amad stay here together which causes some minor arguments over space but they work it out.

Tone jumped out of the truck first. He walked to the back and grabs the buried bags. B stayed inside on his cell explaining to his girl Ashley why he would be out a while longer. White Boy and I exit the truck and head for the front door but before we reach it, I stopped and remind him to grab the guns.

"I'll get y'all guns but you know I can't go to the club without mine," White Boy snapped.

"Man just take the damn guns out. You know Tone will get mad if he finds out you are riding in his shit with your pistol without him knowing."

"Yeah yeah…, but what are we going to do if some niggas pull out some toys and he is the only one blasting back. He'll be mad as hell then."

"Ain't shit going to happen at Keith's man, you know that!" I exclaimed.

White Boy narrowed his eyes at me then turned to the truck. While I waited for White Boy and Tone, I looked up and down the street remembering the days when we played on these streets without having any of our current worries. They strolled up the driveway, talking about the strip club. I interrupted their conversation and give them a plan for us to quickly drop the work off and get to the club. I wanted to have fun but I'm needed at home.

We opened the door hit in the face by a cloud of weed smoke. We all rushed inside eager to go to the strip club especially White Boy.

"What up y'all?" Amad ask staring directly at us. "Where is B?"

"He's still out there," Tone answered.

"Reese I need about a half brick for my people. White Boy are you going to ride with me to drop some of this work off?" Amad said.

"Not tonight. You can handle dealing with them niggas. Shit make them wait we had to." White Boy responded.

"They've been waiting! Shit I've been waiting and I'm ready to get paid."

"Amad, I'm going to give you a whole brick for you to work with because we'll be gone all day tomorrow," I say. "If they're hungry you'll be able to feed them enough for one day."

"Yeah…! Reese half of it will be gone tonight. I'll have the money for you by the end of tomorrow or the next day," Amad said smiling.

"What do y'all have to do tomorrow anyway?"

"We have to hook up with our people to get rid of the weight," I answered.

"All right…!"

"Do you have the money from the other day?" Tone asked.

Amad took a deep breath, "I have eight thousand and I'm about to get the other three."

Tone seemed startled, "Nigga you are already fucking up. You get all of the money from these niggas then put them on again. Give me that shit and when you get the other three give it to White Boy so he can put it in the safe."

Amad stood up. "The money is in the back. How does this new dope look?"

"Tone handed me the bags. I'll put the dope up while I'm back here getting dressed. I'll also grab the eight stacks." White Boy said holding his hands out.

Tone handed the bags over to White Boy. "White Boy give Amad his shit before you put everything up."

White Boy tossed a kilo at Amad.

"Damn this shit looks good!" Amad shouts. "Them Haitians ain't playing. We can triple our money with this shit; I can't wait to blow this shit up."

"Man don't fuck with the shit!" I stress. "Leave it as it is and watch the money stack up. We want the city to know that we have the best dope."

"We're going to eat off this shit. You and White Boy just keep them niggas pushing this shit and we'll supply y'all with what you'll need," Tone add.

"Yeah these muthafuckas have this shit for days. There's no need to get greedy and be fucking over muthafuckas!" I aggressively said.

"All right man, damn. I understand. I'm just saying—" Amad is cut off mid-sentence.

White Boy rushed into the room and interjects, "I have the money and the dope is put up, are y'all ready to see some bitches?"

"Yeah we're ready," I said.

"Shit, let's go!" White Boy shouted.

When we stepped out, I noticed B has climbed into the front passenger seat. He looks at me with a grin telling me he did it purposely. I laugh it off. This was something we did as kids in Keith's many luxury cars.

During the drive toward Keith's club, we're all feeling good. Tone has the speakers blasting and we spit along with the lyrics.

I meditate staring out the passenger window. Hooking up with J was something we needed for a long time. J was a real connect and is reliable to have good dope at all times. Amad and his team were doing their part with helping to move the packs. I had doubted Amad would be able to handle the stress of being a dealer but he is holding it down and getting his money as well. We have dreamed and anticipated for the day when we would be getting real money with a real connect and now we just have to go get it. Damn it feels good!

Suddenly Tone sat up in his seat and turns the volume way down, "Shit y'all the police are right behind me."

"You think the music made him get on us?" B asked.

"No, he just rode out from that street back there. I ain't worried about them, we took everything out." Tone continued to check his rearview mirror.

White Boy leans over and whispers to me. "I didn't take out his pistol inside the house."

I sent him back a look. I quickly get on my toes and think fast, "Man make sure that it's tucked away if you can. Take out the clip and put it on the side of your door. You need to cut that hot shit out bruh!"

"I told you I couldn't go naked. I'm not ever going to get caught slipping without mine."

"Hopefully nothing happens and they're just checking the plates or some silly shit," I said.

The cruiser lights circle on. The lights shine throughout the truck and capture all movement.

"I hate these bitch muthafuckas!" B shouted.

"What do these muthafuckas want? A muthafucka cannot do shit anymore! Can't even breathe out here before one of these muthafuckas is on your ass…!" Tone barks shaking his head.

"Tone I still have my .45 under the seat," White Boy announced.

"What! I thought you had taken everyone's shit out. Why did you bring it anyway to Keith's club?" Tone wondered out loud.

"Bruh you know me."

"Man you know you didn't need to bring it. Don't worry about shit they don't have any reasons to search." Tone add.

"Tone if they do search you know I'll eat whatever happens."

"This might be just a routine stop for some bogus ass reason," I said.

"They can try to do whatever. I'm legit and I'm not letting them search shit! Fuck em!" Tone exclaimed.

White Boy give me the money, you don't need to have all of the money on you just in case." I instructed.

White Boy dug inside his pockets and took out the knots of cash. I grabbed the money and separate it evenly amongst us.

Tone slowly pulled the truck over alongside the street driving over puddles. We waited for the confrontation sitting quiet and still. Five minutes passed and the cruiser remains sitting behind us without movement.

Then a bright ass light shined in on us making it hard to see. The light slowly circulated throughout the car. We all know this is a tactic many police use to be funny. With four black men riding in a new truck, tinted windows, custom paint, and sitting tall, we're prime targets for jealous ass police.

Breaking the silence, the cruiser door slammed shut and the officer walked toward us. He creeps up shining his flashlight on us and on the truck.

I turned my head away from the bright light but White Boy nudges me to look in Tones direction. The officer stood at Tone's door. Tone rolled down the window and begins to answer the cop's questions. I studied the cops facial expressions and body language as they talked. It's strange to see a young black cop alone at this time of night. I could tell the cop is new on the force from his vocabulary. Tone tried to ask for a reason for the stop but the officer managed to ignore him and countered with questions of his own. The officer asked for Tone's proof of insurance and license and while Tone pulled them out to show him, he leans inside. He frowned but changes his facial expression immediately when Tone handed over his information.

He flashed his light on the ID, "I would like for the rest of you gentlemen to pass me your ID's."

We all passed the ID's. He shuffled through them reading them all thoroughly. The officer writes down our information on a note pad and walks back toward his cruiser.

"Man he's on some bullshit! I knew he was going to fuck with us," White Boy exclaimed.

"Relax man I got this." Tone tries to ease White Boy.

"Did y'all muthafuckas see how that bitch looked at us?" B asked.

"Listen y'all if he wanted to do something to us or had something on us he would have called in for back up.," I replied.

"Especially around this way. Cops are on that bullshit real tough just waiting to fuck with some niggas." Tone added.

Seconds later a silver Charger pulls in front of us with a bright blue light flashing from the rear window. This car had to belong to a detective of some sort. The officer climbed out of the cruiser walking past us toward the Charger not once looking our way. He handed over our ID's to the detective with a smile waiting by the door for the detective to step out. The detective stepped out and they walk back to us. The detective stopped at Tone's door while the officer holds a position at the rear with a steady aim.

The detective smiled, "What up fellas I'm Detective Earl Shaw. I apologize for any inconvenience my officer may have given you but he is new on the force. Here are y'all ID's. I know you all are wondering why we made the stop."

"Yes sir we are," Tone stated.

"Well, let me first tell you gentlemen what I do and who I am. You see this here is my district of the city. I have been on the force thirteen years and spent all of it right here. I make sure all business that goes on around here is run correctly just the way I like it."

"What!" White Boy shouted before I nudge him telling him to calm down.

"If you all are entering my district to do any business or dealings, I need to know. I need to know everything that goes on around here and I assume you men are not stupid. Y'all look smart so I want all of you to understand what I'm saying. Now my team really runs this city and if I were y'all I would just comply and tell me where is y'all destination?"

"We're about—" B started.

"Before anyone says a word, if y'all want this to be a quick stop you need to be straight with me. If not I'll call for back up, bring in the dogs and we'll find something to make an arrest. I believe it's best for y'all to be honest."

I took a deep breath before speaking, "Excuse me sir."

"Call me Shaw."

"Well Shaw, I'm not going to bullshit you nor waste your time. We're not here to do any business. We're on our way to a friend's new club to enjoy ourselves," I explained.

"You all are friends of Keith the new strip club owner?"

"Yeah that's our boy," Tone answered.

"Detective we ain't out here to fuck around with any of your shit. We just want to drink a little and spend some money on the bad ass bitches that are waiting for us." White Boy added.

"Tonight is your lucky night. I've known Keith for a while now." He smirks. "Yeah let's just say we know each other very well. I still have his cell phone number if it's the same. I might give him a call. Since you are friends of Keith you are friends of mine. Gentlemen go and enjoy your night but before y'all spend all of your hard earned dope money on them bitches, here is my card just in case y'all find some trouble."

He handed Tone the card with a huge smile on his face. The detective works us dealers to get his extra pay and wanted some money to satisfy his greed.

"Shaw we know what's up and maybe we'll need you one day. We'll call you if we find that trouble you mentioned. I have two grand for your advice and time. We do thank you for the offer and allowing us to be on our way," I say passing the money to Tone who hands it over to Shaw.

Detective Shaw grabbed the cash and stuffs his suit pocket. He looked around then orders the officer to holster his weapon. "I appreciate the donation. Yeah you all have to be Keith's boys. You are Maurice right?" Shaw points at me. I'm going to be watching you and with my protection, you'll never have any trouble with my team. Like I said before y'all look smart. I look forward to doing business together." Shaw walks back to his car. Before pulling off, he signals with his hand for us to call him.

Shaw smashed down on the gas leaving the scene but Tone waits to move until the cruiser turned off its lights and zoomed pass us.

"What the fuck was that about?" Tone said nervously.

"You know how crooked these cops are man. That nigga there we're going to have to watch, he isn't stupid." B countered. You're right. He knows Keith and he knows what we're out here doing. He wants to fuck with us so he can get part of our shit. Fuck that I need every dollar and I know y'all do too!" White Boy protested.

Tone took a glance at the business card and passed it to me.

I placed my fist against my temple and go into deep thought. "We're going to have to talk to Keith about this muthafucka."

"Before we talk to Keith we need to decide what we want to do first," Tone said.

"Tone I'm thinking the same thing even though I don't trust any punk ass cops," B replied. "This is about us not Keith. Keith's done with the game and so much has changed since he's been in it."

"Keith knows more about the game than we'll probably ever know. Trust me Keith has not lost touch with the streets. If Keith has some information on Shaw we definitely need to listen. We need to know who we're fucking with," I responded defensively.

"I agree but I'm just saying that we need to decide on our own and look out for ourselves." Tone tries to rationalize the situation.

"Look we're always going to look out for ourselves first and foremost. To do that, we need as much info on Shaw as possible. Keith will tell us all we need to know about him, then we'll decide if we'll deal with him or not," I said sternly.

"Sounds like a plan," B said.

"Y'all niggas ass crazy as hell but I'm down for whatever," White Boy interjected rolling up a blunt.

"Snake ass cops like Shaw can be a good asset for our operation. With us taking more chances now, we'll need a dirty cop like him on our payroll." Tone pressed.

"You're right Tone but the only thing is we don't know this muthafucka. We have to go about this like we do with everything else," I responded.

"In the meantime, we have to be extra careful and watch each other's back more now. White Boy, you and Amad try to stay out of the way and keep the business flowing. Do not bring any attention to the house. We can't afford any fuck ups," B added.

"I'll make sure he does what he has to do and I'll stay right by his side. Y'all do not have to worry about me. Now can we go inside so we can enjoy some of our hard work?" White Boy countered.

CHAPTER 3

REESE

We pulled up to Keith's at 11 and the club is packed. The whole parking lot is full. It took us a good ten minutes just to get in from the street to the parking lot. Tone had to pump the brakes a few times dodging bad ass chicks walking to the front entrance. The sound of Keisha Cole blasted through the speakers to the parking lot. We didn't have to worry about finding a parking spot because Keith had five V.I.P spots. Tone pulled right up to Keith's new Mercedes.

The line was out of the door and although it's a men club there is a lot of women. Keith's club is bright looking like it should be on the Vegas strip. He had a lot of the fixings with valet parking and a V.I.P. entrance. We all had got out of the truck feeling good headed to V.I.P. A group of cocktail waitresses stood behind the four huge bouncers to intimidate everybody. Before we had a chance to be greeted, a bouncer had told us some ladies have asked about us. The bouncers looked like they were in Special Forces. Whatever Keith puts his money into he expects the best.

The inside of the club is top notch; white leather seats, six gold stripper poles, glass ceilings and glass stage, four pool tables with see through balls, and a bar with any drink possible. The waitresses escorted us to our private V.I.P. room, where there were bottles of Cristal on ice, one-way glass mirrors, and a few love seats for us to relax.

"Y'all, I think we should invest in a club." Tone suggested taking a seat.

"It would be nice but it takes a lot to run a club," B replied.

White boy adds, "This club is all right. Keith had to put close to a million in here."

"Excuse me but what's your name Miss?" I asked a dark-skinned skinny sister.

"Jasmine" she responded.

"Do me a favor and let Keith know we're here" I asked.

I'll go get him cutie. But trust me he already knows."

I handed her a bill and she thanks me asking if we need anything else.

"Yeah Ma before you bring Keith can you ask that bouncer who was talking to us to come here?"

"Sure Hun," Jasmine said cheerfully walking out the room.

"Tone, it's a good idea for us to get a club but not a strip club. We'll make more money with something for everybody," I said. B interjected, "We'll need someone legit to put their name on it so nothing happens. Tone how big was the building?"

"It's a nice size. I think it used to be an old factory. It will cost us," Tone answered.

"Yeah Christian can do it! We'll just make sure things run smoothly. With this new money we can get it no matter what bruh," White Boy said cheerfully.

"So we're all on this?" I asked.

"Yeah…!" They all shout together.

"I'm going to call my little brother," I said pulling out my cell phone.

While on my phone I'm watching White Boy becoming excited. He was counting his money in which I'm assuming he's figuring how much he's going to spend.

The Bouncer approached us. "Jazz told me that one of y'all wanted to see me."

"Yeah man you said when we came in that some ladies were asking about us," White boy said. Yeah there's three chick's next door in the main V.I.P. room that asked me about Reese."

"Okay Reese I see you got them on deck," Tone laughed.

B asked, "Man do you know who they could be?"

"I'm about to go see who are they. It's probably just some chic's from the hood," White Boy interjected.

"Nah, I don't know who they could be. Only one who knows that I'm here is Diana." I say wondering who these girls could be.

"Let's send a bottle of "Ace of Spades" over there," Tone suggested.

"I'll let Jazz know," The bouncer says leaving the room. Y'all don't want to go to see who we're sending an expensive bottle to?" White Boy questioned.

"Yes I do but let them get the bottle first. Besides, we need to decide what we're going to do about Detective Shaw," I replied.

White Boy replied, "Man I don't give a fuck. I'm just ready to fuck with some bitches."

"This shit comes first man," B challenged.

Keith enters the room, "Fellas, what's good? How do y'all like my place?" He stands with a smile on his face.

"Just who we need to talk to about this shit…!" I shouted.

"What?" Keith erases his smile.

"Your place is nice. You have some badass dancers also. White Boy and I are about to get a closer view by the stage so we can get on something," Tone answered.

"Just hold on. I'll make sure these ladies take well care of y'all," Keith said.

B approached him, "On the way over here we were stopped by a cop and a detective."

Keith's eyes grew with excitement, "A detective."

"Yeah man. The muthafucka said he knows you. His name is Shaw," I said.

Keith brushed his beard with his hand. "I know him. That is the wrong but right kind of cop. He will help you in key situations if y'all know what I mean. He used to let me know when the cops wanted to hit one of my spots here in the city. He informed me on the snitches and my competitions business."

I looked Keith dead in the eye. "So do you suggest that we fuck with him?"

Keith circles the room with his eyes. "Listen up, if y'all decide to fuck with him use him for your benefit not his. He is a piece of shit but a damn good cop. Y'all work it out and think it through carefully. Never doubt your first thought and trust in not just your own but each other instincts."

"That's what we'll do. I'm glad you gave us your advice on the nigga it was a lot of help," I said.

"So what's up y'all? I'm with whatever y'all want to do," Tone added.

White Boy sat silently staring at the women walking by.

"Yes we can use him. I have a plan for a job to use the detective for our benefit," B replied.

"Y'all stay smart and be careful. This is big business for y'all that will make y'all or break y'all. James is a well-respected man and he does not take kindly to any heat. Keep business good between y'all and y'all can live a good life," Keith says.

B walked toward me pulling his cell phone out, "Let me have Shaw's number."

I gave B the business card and he programs the number into his phone. "Keith who are them girl's next door?" I asked.

"With all of this police talk I almost forgot about the pretty ladies next door. That's Simone and her two friends," Keith chuckled.

"She was asking that big ass bouncer who'd just left out questions about me."

Keith laughs harder, "You must be talking about Rocks big ass."

"What do her friends look like?" White Boy questioned.

"White Boy I know you'll like Peaches. She is light skin like you, with an ass shaped just like her name."

White Boy licks his lips in thought.

"All of them are nice," Keith continued.

White Boy rubs his hands together with excitement.

"Keith what's up with Simone?" I inquired.

"Simone is out here doing the damn thing. She is riding good and she dress very well. The girl hustles but I honestly do not know what. She hasn't come to me asking about you but I'm sure she will if you don't go speak to her."

Tone busted out in laughter, "That nigga ain't going to talk to her or any other chick. He is on lock down. That niggas dick belongs to Diana."

Keith turned for the door and stands still pointing toward the direction of the floor, "Reese, there they are now. You need me to do the introduction?"

"I'm good. I'll go and introduce myself but not to get at her. I want to find out why she's interested in me and what she knows about us."

"I'll catch y'all later. I need to get out here and check on my money. Jasmine will be back to keep the bottles coming and make sure y'all enjoy yourselves with my lovely ladies. We all are celebrating tonight right?"

"Hell yeah…!" Tone and White Boy yell in unison.

"I'll send Jasmine in a minute with some girls."

"Keith, I want her on stage to come for me when you send the girls,"

White Boy requested, staring at the dancer clapping her ass on stage.

Keith laughed, "Which one man?"

"The one with the white thong on. Damn she's working that shit," White Boy answered.

"Okay, I see. Look at those fools mesmerized by her. When she is done I'll tell her. All right fellas I have to go."

When Keith exit the room, my attention went directly to Simone. Keith didn't lie about her beauty. I studied her body as she and her friends find a table. She sat down with elegance and class, crossing her legs and holding her glass. A sexy dress and a nice pair of strapped heels that swirl around her leg like a snake show her class. The dress showed her sexy legs and the thickness of her yellow thighs. She reminded me of a thicker Monica the R&B singer. Her gorgeous looked and elegance stood out from her friends although Peaches is running a close race. Now I was more than motivated to get to know her.

"White Boy are you ready to have a good time?" I asked.

"You know I am!"

"Buy the bar out. Get some girl and let her go home feeling like she shut it down tonight."

"I definitely can do that Reese!"

"Y'all niggas are crazy. Reese you done let the wrong nigga show out in here," B joked.

"Like Keith said it's time to celebrate," Tone stated.

White Boy leaves the room and walks over to the bar. I watch him laughing at his excitement but catch Peaches and the other girl looking in his direction. I'm wondering if they're looking for us all in general. Keith joins White Boy at the bar and they raise their glasses.

The bartender rung a loud bell catching everyone's attention stopping the music. The DJ announces, "The bar is now free so ladies drink up and y'all ballers share some of that dope money on these fine ass ladies in here working hard tonight. Y'all fake ass ballers recognize how real niggas do it. Shouts out to White Boy and the whole I75 crew."

Most of the crowd also raises their drinks to show appreciation. White Boy follows Jasmine as she brings a bucket of champagne and six strippers. They go to work but I didn't get involved because I'm drawn to Simone.

I looked over at Tone and he has two pair of titties in his face. One chick was bouncing on his lap and the other was kissing all over his neck. White Boy was being White Boy slapping ass, sucking on titties, playing with their pussy, and teasing them with his money. B was standing against the wall throwing money on the floor while a naked girl bends over and rolls her ass.

My phone caught me by surprise vibrating on my hip. I receive a text from Diana. "What up I've been out of the tub for an hour and I'm still wet," she says. With all of this ass around me, I'm ready to fuck now. I'm fantasizing about fucking the shit out of Diana watching her facial expressions with each thrust. I need to call her now so she'll be ready soon as I open the door. Slowly, I crept out of the V.I.P room and notice Simone and her girls are gone. Maybe they went back to their room or maybe the restroom. Remembering another car in one of the V.I.P parking spots. With us being the only VIPs' her car has to be the Audi A6. I decided to escape all of this ass and noise in order to get away and call Diana without her asking any questions.

"Reese, where are you about to go?," White Boy wonders with a confused look on his face.

"Diana texted me, so I need to get out and call her real quick," I replied.

"I can't believe this shit. We have all of this ass around us and a bad ass bitch is here who wants to fuck with you and you worried about the in house," White Boy presses. Nigga that's my woman! Fuck these bitches. She'll be there when everything is gone."

Tone excuses himself from the girls. "Here man you need the keys? Fuck what he talking about."

"I'll be all right bruh."

"Are you sure that you are okay?" B asks.

"Yeah I'll be okay, just calling her back real quick before she is on one."

Attempting to exit the club, people are thanking me for the drinks and trying to tell me who they were but that shit goes in one ear and out the other. When I finally step out and walk over to Tone's truck, I touch the screen and I have two new picture messages. The first picture was of Diana taking a bubble bath. Next picture showed me she was not lying about how wet she was. I'm excited to get home. I switched over to call her.

"What's up baby? I'll be home in a few more minutes, we're now finishing up. I love those pictures. You're so nasty."

"Stop flirting and get your butt home. I'm horny and I'm lonely," she says sadly.

"I'll be home soon."

"Love you baby." Diana closed.

"Love you too baby."

A female's voice comes from the darkness, "Aw, that is so sweet. I wish I had a man like you."

"Who's that?" I question even though I have a guess as to who it is.

Simone was sitting in her car this whole time. I felt as if the FEDs were listening to me. She rolls her window down further so that I can get a good look at her.

"Why don't you come here and find out who I am?"

"Nah, I don't walk up to anybody car in the darkness not knowing who they are. How about you come over here to me?"

"It's kind of cold out there," Simone playfully whined.

"You are right, that's why I'm about to go in here and get my boys so that we can go."

"Leaving early, huh? Well hold on here I come..."

Simone hopped out the car after quickly talking to her friend. She struts over to me rapidly trying to resist from smiling.

"Thanks for coming over to me, a lot of women wouldn't have done that."

"I'm way different from a lot of women."

I stared at her. "Are you going to tell me your name?"

Simone stood beside me looking in the direction of her car. "My name is Simone and that's my girl Cherish. We're waiting on our girl Peaches. Who's in there bullshiting. She needs to bring her ass on. I'm ready to go to bed."

"I heard that. Did you enjoy yourself?"

"I sure did now," she said with a flirtatious look.

"Oh yeah. My boy Keith did his damn thing with this."

"Yes he did. This club is one of the best. I came out tonight to support my girl who is dancing tonight. Thanks for the bottle."

"Aw, it wasn't anything. The crew and I were here to celebrate."

"I guess that's how you and your boys get down."

I chuckled, "What do you mean?"

"Buying the bar and sending some girls y'all don't know an expensive bottle of champagne," she answers.

"Keith told us there were some pretty women in the other V.I.P so we decided to treat y'all. It was nothing."

Simone playfully slaps me on the chest. "I hear you are a ladies man and you know how to handle your business."

"Hold on, hold on, hold on. You know a lot about me and all I know is your name."

"That's your fault. I have been here with my girls for over three hours now and I catch you out in the parking lot. I even asked the bouncer Rock to tell you I wanted to meet you."

I looked over toward the exit and B was trying to get my attention. I excuse myself and ask her to wait for me while I talk to B. She just nods holding her arms tight from the chill.

"I just got off the phone with Shaw. I'm making him check on some people for us. He is only asking for us to pay him thirty-five hundred and he took the two from earlier as a down payment."

"That's good news. We have to listen to Keith and remember that Shaw is a snake and use him to our benefit."

"You are right. Let's go back in here and get these niggas so we can be ready to go to work tomorrow."

"Hold up bruh. I'll be right in there I'm trying to get her."

Simone has already jumped back in the car and I feel as if this will be my last chance. I turned away from B and run to Simone's driver door. I had caught her by surprise and asked if she would care to stepped out and talk to me for a moment.

"My fault I had to handle business with my boy. He is ready to go as much as I am. I know you are cold and want to go so how about we get together Friday and I can get to know you better?"

"Okay ladies' man. Let me put my number in your phone so you can call me. I hope I can see you Friday."

Before getting back inside, she gives me a hug and I smell her cucumber melon body spray. The scent and the softness of her body is getting me hard as hell. I hope she didn't notice the bulge in my pants but she did pull me closer to her. This girl is a freak and really want a nigga to take her down. After our hug, she turned away and dipped back inside her car. I keep my eyes on her ass.

I rushed back over to B where he stood cracking up at my actions. Him and I talked about that ass before reentering the club.

Walking in we busted out laughing at the sight of White Boy acting a fool with the stripper he wants so bad. White Boy had two fistfuls of cash and tossing them all over the stripper. The stripper was very agile bouncing her ass off his lap then flipping onto the stage into a split. She begun to bounce her ass on the stage floor allowing White Boy to slap her ass and cover her with cash. Taking White Boys hand, she let him feel on her pussy, giving him a quick tease.

I walked up behind Tone who is drinking from a champagne bottle.

"Y'all ready to go yet?" I asked knowing they want to stay longer.

"I am but that nigga ain't. He told Keith to keep her on the stage so he can have his personal show," Tone laughed.

White Boy notices we're standing behind him. "What up? You see this Reese. This is how I get down."

"Bruh I see you but it's time to head out. We have shit to do tomorrow remember."

White Boy throws the rest of his cash on stage. "Damn man it is still early. You see she's on me."

"We have to go man," B said defending me.

The stripper looked disappointed as she picks up her bra and cash but blows White Boy a kiss good-bye. I threw my arm around him and try to get him focused on what is important but he still has an attitude. I ignored him and pull my phone out texting Diana telling her I'm on my way.

We all enjoyed ourselves at Keith's and talked about the night on our way home. Tone drove White Boy home first. I would be home inside of Diana in no time.

CHAPTER 4

REESE

Finally I arrived home. I felt a sense of relief. I hurry out of the truck and rush for the door. I wanted to feel the warmth of my girl's touch and comfort of our bed. Today had worn me out but tomorrow is promising. We have to drop most of the weight off to our regulars and maybe some to these new niggas. I'm not going to stress whether these guys are good to do business with. B had the detective running a check on them to see if they are credible. Now all I want to do is take care of home. I have a good woman but lately I've been distant worried about how we'll continued our way of life and make it better for the future.

Before today, the crew and I would travel back and forth out of state to buy some weight. We decided the smart thing to do would be to stay a few days before riding back out. During our stays, I would buy Diana some designer handbags, clothes, heels, just to sooth her when I walk in the door. Although she isn't materialistic and never wants the gifts, I bought them anyway maybe to ease myself knowing what I'm doing is wrong. All she wanted was for me to be home with her and leave the game alone. I tried to explain that it's not as easy as it sound but she doesn't understand. Diana believed that with her job and the money I have saved we'll have more than enough. I knew we're not even close but with this new connect we can get what we want fast. We had a deep conversation recently about my income but I assured her Keith had set us up with a connect and everything would be better allowing me to be home more often. My news didn't relieve her stress but she accepted it.

Unlocking the door I heard the soft sound of R&B music coming from inside. I opened the door slowly instantly smelling the aroma candles lit around the house. Across the couch laid a black lingerie outfit. I quickly turn off my phone and plugged the charger to it. I hurried for the stairs, but soon I placed a foot on the stairs, there she was standing at the top totally naked. The candle light flickered off her body showing her caramel skin. I could tell that she just wiped down her body with oil.

"Did you have fun with your friends tonight while I was here alone waiting on you?"

"Diana why are you trying to start some shit? You didn't put this all together just for me to come home and argue."

"I'm pampering myself since no one wants to do it for me!" Diana snapped.

"Oh here you go."

"You're right here I go! I was blowing your phone up earlier! You could've answered!" She barks jerking her head with much attitude.

I briefly took my eyes off her body and looked up at the ceiling. "You know I was doing business with the fellas. I told you today we had to meet up with Keith's people."

"I know you need to do what you have to but sometimes I need you." She said with a soft tone changing her attitude.

I climbed a few steps creeping up slowly. "I'm just trying to pay the bills and take care of you."

"We're okay. I want you to stop."

"I can't. Not yet. This is my only way I know how to get paid and my boys are my family," I speak sincerely.

"I want to be your family. I want us to be married," she cried.

Standing before her I spoke softly, "With the money I'm going to make, we'll soon get married. I just need to find a way to turn it into legal money. The crew and I were discussing that also. We're going to buy our own club and try to leave the dope game alone. Stop crying, damn!"

Diana stepped down to me and grabs my face, "Promise me this will all be over soon. I can't imagine myself going through this alone."

I looked at her confused, "Going through what?"

"That's what I wanted to tell you earlier."

She wiped her eyes, "I don't want you to get mad but I left work early today."

"Why?"

"Just listen. I felt sick and threw up. I went to see my doctor. After I took a urine test they told me I'm ten weeks pregnant."

"Hold up, what?" I said amazed.

"Yeah I knew I was gaining weight because my pants weren't fitting well but I didn't dream it was because I'm pregnant."

"I don't believe it! You're having my baby. I'll change I promise. I'll answer my phone for now on."

I wiped away her tears with my thumbs and give her a soft kiss. Quickly I picked her up off her feet and carried her into the bedroom. Diana and I exchanged kisses all the way to the bed. I gently laid her across the bed and kiss her breasts. She reached around my waist but I stop her and slowly take all my clothes off for her pleasure.

Standing before her naked, she sits up and takes my shaft inside her mouth. Diana is handling her business very well causing me to lose balance so I step back just enough to pull away. She laughed as I push her back onto the bed.

I climbed on top of her and go right back to sucking on her size D breast. Swirling my tongue over her nipples then gradually scrolling it down her stomach. I teased her with soft kisses around her stomach and thighs before I spread her thighs wide open and taste everything in-between. Diana begun to squirm all over the bed twisting the sheets. I rapidly flicked my tongue on her clit causing her to have a huge orgasm. Diana let out a loud scream and tensed up forcing me to stop.

She looked at me embarrassed but invites me inside her. The moment I'd thrust inside she moans loudly and screws her face up. Her pussy is so wet allowing me to slide in and out with long deep strokes. After a few minutes of long-stroking I felt my orgasm building so I rapidly pound the pussy. I'd threw her legs up on my shoulders and dig in deeper feeling everything inside her. I'm pounding her so hard I ignored her moans and thrust more rapidly inside watching her breast bounce around. I'd slow down my pace and begin to grind letting out all I'd built up inside me. We continued to make love for hours both sharing multiple orgasms.

In the early hours of the morning the house phone rings. I don't want to answer it but any second Diana will wake up from the disturbing ring. I rolled over turning on my side checking the caller ID. Its B. Diana stirs and begged me not to answer. She wanted me to stay home with her for the day. I reminded her that I have to go to work today but I promised her that when I got home it will be all about her. I picked up the phone on the third ring.

"Get your ass up nigga," B playfully said.

"Man I'm still tired. I enjoyed every bit of last night."

"Yeah Keith's spot is the shit. Do you need me to come get you so we can handle business today?"

"Nah, I'll be okay. I have something to take care of first or should I say somebody to take care of," I chuckled.

"Man don't be bullshiting!" B orderd...

"I'll be there soon just give me about thirty minutes," I said ending the call.

"Are you going to stay with me?" Diana begged.

"Babe I can't. You just be ready to leave when I come home. I have a surprise for you."

She rolled over onto her side facing away from me. "Reese call me when you are on your way. Do you want me to get up and fix you something to eat?"

"No, baby you don't have to do that. You know what? I'm going to make you something. You just relax. Matter of fact I want you to go spend some time at the day spa while I'm gone. I should be home by eight o'clock. I'll make dinner reservations at that Italian restaurant you like."

"Oh baby that will be nice... I can't wait!" she replies with excitement.

I walked into the kitchen opening the refrigerator but cannot find anything quick to fix for her. I had to give her something to eat that is quick and will also satisfy her. I open up the cabinet and fix her favorite bowl of cereal.

I took the bowl of cereal to her laughing the whole way. She sat up in the bed and laughs at me. Before digging in we shared a kiss and I again remind her about tonight's event. Although she liked to drive my Escalade I had told her that was I driving it today. I pulled up to the spot and everyone was there. I was surprised to see them before me. Slowly entering the house and White Boy has already sorted the bags. We had to hook up with our people here in our city and with our Columbus boys. They both wanted more than their regular amounts to make up to their customers for our absence. The city crew normally got three to four bricks but now they want five and the Columbus boys want four. We also had to meet up with Amad's people. If everything went as planned we could be going through ten to fifteen a week.

B pulled me aside and informs me that he had spoken with Detective Shaw and that Shaw said that Amad's new friends are okay to do business with. Amad overheard and replied to B's comment saying that we wasted our time doing a background check.

"Tone you want to go see what these niggas are about first for ourselves?" White Boy asks.

"Yeah…, Amad call your people and set it up. Tell them to meet us at the park," Tone instructed.

"Amad I also need you to hook up with Detective Shaw and give him fifteen hundred," B orders.

"Why in the hell are we paying a detective?" Amad wondered.

"Man just do it. I'm texting you his number now," B snapped.

"Y'all muthafuckas ready to do our job?" Tone said.

"Who's driving?" B asked.

"I will," I jingle the keys in my hand.

A few steps behind me White Boy shouts, "Reese don't forget to get your gun and I have some clips. Everything is in the safe."

"I don't need any extra clips; just my gun will do."

I jumped onto my trunk, Tone was on his cell phone already handling business talking to our city crew. I heard him telling them that we have to charge more for a price of twenty five thousand because of the quality. I loved it when others in my crew handle business other than me.

White Boy was in the back locking and loading. All I can do is thank God he's on my side and not against me. B is on the phone talking to his girl again arguing about the same shit Diana and I went through this morning.

I noticed I was not focused so I quickly get my head right. Anything can happen when you're doing a drug deal. While driving, I considered how this money will be spent in the near future. I thought about our conversation at Keith's about getting a club. This would be our first step to getting some legitimate money and putting the game behind. I called my little brother Christian and inform him on our plans about getting the club and putting the business under his name. Christian gladly accepts. He had a good business sense and ambition but I keep his ass away from the game. I gave him all he could want plus more just to stay away. I told him I'll soon quit dealing and focus on the club but he isn't happy for me. I didn't understand and I'm not going to force him to understand either. I let him know we have found a nice size building that will hold a large crowd. The building was for sale and after we contact the owner we'll need him to sign off on the paperwork. I figured Keith would be able to help us get our liquor license. Christian shot me ideas for what he had in mind to promote the club. He said two of his boys could come through and help get the building together. Before I ended the call I told him I'll have Tone meet with him and the owner to check out the building.

"Y'all, that was my little brother and he'll help with the club. Tone can you meet with him and get in contact with the owner tomorrow?"

"Yeah…" Tone nodded.

"Amad texted me and said he paid Shaw the money. He also spoke with his people from school and they said they would meet us at the park." White Boy interjects.

"All right, you and I'll see if these muthafuckas are real or not," Tone exclaimed.

We met up with the Columbus crew first and everything was run smoothly. We got all we need and they got what they want and hit the highway to make their money back. Next we meet with our other crew. They have their scales ready and money set aside for us. We allowed them to weigh up the dope while B and I counted the cash. We could never let our guards down. Before we drove away, they asked us to have another order ready for them as soon as possible. They complement how good the work was and looked forward to our next meeting.

Today was a good day and we all make a profit. After dropping Tone and White Boy off to meet Amad's people, B and I went to the bank to get some more money so we can treat our girls.

On the way to B's house I spotted a travel agency advertising a trip to the Bahamas. This might be the perfect solution for Diana and I to get away and for her a peace of mind. A vacation could bring us together and strengthen our relationship.

I pulled up to the travel agency, sitting down with the agent and discuss my travel needs. She helped me book the tickets for two. We received airfare to Miami and a seven-day vacation at a hotel in the Bahamas. I made the reservations for early next month when the weather becomes warmer so I could handle business in the meantime.

Putting the tickets in my back pocket leaving out the agency, I was so happy to know that Diana and I are getting away. We quickly arrived at B's house and he hopped out heading for the door.

B rushed inside the house to get Ashley giving me the opportunity to call Diana.

"Baby where are you? Are you home yet?" I asked wondering if she's still pampering herself.

"I just walked in. You're going to love the dress I bought today. I'll wear it tonight."

The thought of her dressed up excites me. "I can't wait. I'm waiting for B and Ashley. Soon as they hop in, I'll be on my way."

"I'll be ready," Diana replies.

A few minutes later, I sped to get home. I couldn't wait to see my girl tonight. When I pulled in our driveway I notice my front door is open.

Diana is too scared to leave the door open so I grabbed my 9mm as I run to the door. Somebody had broken into my house and I have to protect my woman.

Diana let out a horrible scream and then a loud bang hits the floor. I rushed to the bedroom door and notice B standing behind me with his pistol ready. I pushed the door open.

Diana stood in front of the dresser mirror. "Oh Reese you scared me!" She said frightfully jumping back.

"You scared me. I thought something was wrong." I put my gun away tucking it in my waistband.

"It is! I'm fat that's what's wrong. I wanted to look good for you tonight but I'm a fat cow. I look funny in this dress," she whines.

"You're fine baby. I don't even see the extra weight. Calm down and trust me, you look good."

"You don't have to lie to me in order for me to feel good."

"I'm not. You look good as hell." I throw my arms around her.

Diana saw the gun and wonders why I have it on me when we're going out together. I gave her a bullshit answer which she does not accept and she gets on me again asking me to stop. She tells me she wants to move further away from all the city life. Dianna told me about a nice community with a few houses for sale. I told her we'll look at a house in our price range. She said she'll go online to check but knows the homes start at two hundred and fifty thousand dollars.

I took her to a fancy restaurant east of town where the upper class resided. In the outside shopping mall area is an upscale jewelry store. When I drove pass the restaurant and pulled in front of the jewelry store, her face shows total surprise.

"Boy you know I need to eat," she playfully snapped.

"Reese, what are we doing here?" Ashley questioned with a blank look.

"Girl just get out!" B interjected.

I hurried out of the truck and around to open the passenger door. I received a silly look from her, which was understandable because I didn't often do this.

When we enter the store B and Ashley walk over to look at some earrings and necklaces. I took Diana by the hand and lead her to a seat in front of the wedding rings. Her gaze was glued to the wedding sets.

"Hello. Can I help you?" An older white lady asks.

"You're a size 7 right?" I asked.

"Yes but what does this mean Reese?"

"This means that I'm serious about us. I want you. I want us to be a family."

Tears flow down her face. I gently place a kiss on her lips as she wipes her tears. Ashley breaks away from B and walks over to share in Diana's excitement.

I requested for the saleswoman to set out their best wedding rings on the jewelry case. While the girls were looking through the rings, I slid my credit card to the manager standing behind the cash register. Most jewelry stores kept the expensive jewelry in the back and I requested for him to bring that out for Diana. He gave us a sneaky grin.

Before the manager could walk to the back, B asked him if he could make customized jewelry for us.

"How much are we talking about?" the jeweler asked.

"I have sixty thousand for a black diamond I75/70 charm if you can make it," I challenged.

"I can have that made soon. I'll need a down payment to get started."

"I would like to get a good deal on a blue diamond ring," B add.

We pulled out our lose money to get the process started. The jeweler gave us his business card and private number. B and I walked over to the ladies and join them on making a decision between two rings. Diana complained about the prices but I assured her not to worry. I told her she can have whichever one she wants and remind her that today was all about her. She decided to pick a four carat princess cut ring. B bought Ashley a three carat bracelet.

After we make our purchases, we walked to the restaurant where I asked the hostess to allow me to speak with the manager. When the manager arrived, I whispered to him that I would like to get the best wine, a good seat and their best hospitality. The manager stood there silent until I placed two hundred dollars in his hand. We were shown to our seats and are immediately greeted by a waiter with a bottle of red wine and glasses. Diana loved all of this attention.

After eating dinner we shared the news about Diana's pregnancy. An excited Ashley congratulated her. B laughed knowing what's to come. I stared at Diana while she's talking to Ashley. I did love the dress on her. The dress complimented her curves just right. We enjoyed the rest of the night talking about our futures and more about the coming baby.

CHAPTER 5

REESE

None of us knew what to think when Amad told us about this new crew. With meeting anyone new in order to do business with we have to check them out. There are not too many crews in our city we didn't know about. Let alone, a crew who's buying weight. White Boy and Tone wanted to find out what had happened with their last connect. If everything was cool like Amad and Shaw said we'll be moving a lot of weight fast and our income will expand. If things didn't go as planned they'll be dealing with some crazy ass niggas who are itching to shoot.

Tone and White Boy sat at the park waiting for Amad's boys to show. With school in session there aren't any kids around to distract them.

"White Boy. Was that Detective Shaw's?" Tone nodded in the direction of a car speeding by.

"Yeah I think it was," White Boy answered.

Tone checks the time on his watch. "Didn't Amad tell you he met with him already?"

"Yeah, he said that a few hours ago."

"I never saw that muthafucka riding around here before. I wonder if something is up," Tone said.

"Me neither. Think this is a setup?"

Tone shakes his head. "Why would Amad set us up? He knows we're just meeting them and we don't have any dope on us. But Shaw might be up to something. I don't trust him."

"We can pop all of the muthafuckas. I don't give a fuck!" White Boy shouted.

"That must be them." Tone pointed to an SUV.

"Why do these niggas want to get on with us? They're riding good." White Boy wondered.

"There's a lot going on today."

"Nothing my .45 can't fix," White Boy pulls back on the hammer.

"Let me talk to these niggas but if you feel something is wrong, I want you to handle your business."

Two men stepped out of the SUV and leaned against the hood. Tone honks his horn. The two men start to walked over and halfway White Boy hops out. He patted them both down. White Boy ushered one inside the passenger seat and the other climb in the back followed by White Boy. White Boy didn't trust these muthafuckas at all.

Tone asked how they had met Amad and what happened between them and their last connect. White Boy sat quietly with his hands folded over the gun. They answer Tone's questioned without hesitation. Their story adds up to what Amad said.

Tone decided to do business with them. Jumping right into it they want to buy five bricks every week and didn't complain about the price White Boy gives them.

White Boy's phone started to ring. He pulls it out of his pocket. "Hello. This is Amad. Y'all can go ahead and leave. We'll get with y'all tomorrow." They exit Tone's truck and pulled off.

Tone and I watch them leave from our sight before we leave ourselves. Tone looks in all directions before deciding on which direction to take making sure that we're not being followed.

"What up? We're just finishing things up with your boys." White Boy said.

"Now that y'all are done doing private investigation work, I need you to put some real work in with me."

"What up?"

"Some of my people fucked up some money."

"What the fuck! I don't want to know how much. I just want to get these niggas!" White Boy spat balling his fist.

"Don't say anything to Tone because he'll call Reese and B. We can handle this ourselves," Amad instructed.

"Yeah whatever, you just be ready. We're about to pull up."

"What is that all about?" Tone asks with laughter believing that Amad has done something stupid…

"Man his people fucked up some more money but I'll handle it."

"If y'all need me I'll go with y'all," Tone said pulling into the driveway.

"We'll handle these niggas. You worry about the building. We have to get that."

"All right I'll talk to you later. I'm calling Christian now," Tone said backing out.

White Boy rapidly ran inside the house and Amad is loading bullets into his .38 pistol. White Boy runs to his room and puts on a pair of gloves and a fitted baseball cap to hide his profile. White Boy fels as if he is responsible for the loss and that Amad's crew is being disrespectful and didn't know whose money they're fucking with.

Riding pass the young crew spot, White Boy checked out their cars knowing that they're getting a lot of money from cooking the dope up. White Boy speeds by roaring the pipes on his '72 Cutlass, turns the corner and drives through the dirty alley. White Boy and Amad hear loud music coming from the house. White Boy thinks to himself they will catch them totally off guard.

They entered through the fence but two muscular pit bulls are on chains sitting guard. Amad pulled out his pistol and place a single shot in each of the dog's head. White Boy charged for the back door. Two kicks and the door is opened. Amad rushes inside first. He noticed a few ounces of cocaine laying on the kitchen counter. They have dirty scales, sandwich bags, measuring jars, and cocaine everywhere. Amad and White Boy crept on opposite sides of the walls entering the living room. Three of the crew members are smoking weed, drinking, and talking shit to each other while they play a dice game.

"I'm about to lay them down. I want you to check the rest of the house for our dope or money. If a muthafucka breathes wrong you should blast his ass," White Boy whispered.

"I just want to get in and out."

White Boy pointed with his gun in the direction he wanted Amad to go. He crept behind the three and slapped one in the back of his head with the gun. The guy slumped over instantly. In shock the other two reach for the sky. White Boy stormed over to the tall skinny guy and slapped him hard to the face causing blood to pour from his cheek. The last youngster begeds for mercy asking White Boy to spare him.

Amad took the house by storm, checking all the down stair rooms. He ran out one of the rooms with a department store bag and tossed it at White Boy. Amad slowed his pace and start creeping upstairs. Amad overheard the third youngster told White Boy that is friend is upstairs. White Boy forced him into the kitchen to fill the bag with the dope. While White Boy was keeping an eye on him he is checking the other two youngsters' pockets. Amad reached the top of the stairs and hears a girl inside moaning. He took a peep inside and the girl is on top of his boy riding the shit out of his dick. Amad accidentally pushed the door open causing it to get her attention. Amad gave her a smile and continued to

57

watch her do her thing. White Boy yelled upstairs rushing him to hurry. Amad rushed over to the bed and pulled the youngster away from her, with the gun staring him down. She tried to grab her shirt to cover herself but Amad shouted at her making her walk down stairs naked also. Amad walked down the stairs with one hand on the back of the youngsters' neck and the pistol to his head. Amad shouted at him asking for the money or the rest of the dope. The youngster looked at White Boy like he don't know what Amad is talking about. Amad asked him again before getting closer to White Boy knowing that from the look of his friend White Boy wasn't playing. He told Amad that the money was upstairs between the mattress and the rest of the work is in a dresser. The youngster tried to question Amad but quickly is shut up by the .38 down his throat. Amad looked over to White Boy but he is staring down the girl. Amad ordered her to go upstairs and get the money and dope.

"Do she look familiar to you?" White Boy asked watching her hurry up the stairs.

"Nah. I ain't never seen her before. Fuck that bitch! I better grab all of that shit so we can get the fuck out of here," Amad exclaimed.

"I know that bitch from somewhere. I don't know her name but I know her face. Shit I know her body." White Boy replies pointing his gun up the stairs.

Boom! Boom! The girl shot two shots at White Boy narrowly missing his head. Without hesitation he shot his whole clip hitting her multiple times. Her naked body tumbled down the stairs. White Boy leap over her lifeless body and took the stairs two at a time until reaching the bedroom. White Boy fpond the stash and throws everything into a plastic bag before rushing back down. White Boy threatened the youngsters' to keep their mouth shut or he'll be back. Amad was nowhere in sight.

White Boy exit the house and heard the sirens becoming closer. He tried to remain calm and speed walks to the car. He threw the bag at Amad in the passenger seat. Before pulling out, he puts the .45 inside the glove compartment.

All of a sudden the naked youngster comes out shooting. White Boy slammed down on the gas dodging potholes in the alley then barely missing a patrol car. He turned the next corner speeding up the street getting the attention of other patrol cars in the area. The patrol cars chased him throughout the neighborhood until they corner him.

Amad jumped out with the bag running through backyards and alleyways but White Boy doesn't have a chance of escaping. Officers are already outside their cars with guns aimed on him. White Boy sat still thinking his days on the streets are over.

Suddenly out of nowhere, silver Charger emerged.

Detective Shaw barge through the cops then walk toward White Boy, where he stood with his hands in the air.

"Turn off your engine and put your hands outside the window," Shaw ordered.

White Boy complied.

"Now I want you to take your right hand and open the door." Shaw steps closer to the passenger door.

"Back down! I'll handle the situation!" he ordered the officers.

White Boy steps out the car and assumes the position. Shaw began to pat him down.

"I knew you were shady and wasn't going to help us get out of shit," White Boy said.

"You got yourself into a lot of shit back there. Now if you don't calm the hell down I might not be able to help you. From the scene back there you are looking at life easily. I need you to help me so I'm going to ask you some questions."

"Man I don't talk to the police."

"You want to face another detective who wants to put your black ass away for life? I bet after they check your car they will find the murder weapon."

White Boy stands tall, breathing real heavy. He wishes he had gotten out of the car blasting. "I'll beat the case. Niggas beat murder cases every day. By the time I get to the county I'll have the best lawyer in Ohio working on my shit."

"Listen, I'm trying to help you. We have witnesses who saw you leave the scene. It didn't look good. Now you can get a lawyer but I'm telling you, without my help you'll still do some time. I knew you don't want that."

"Take me to jail and save me the bullshit."

Detective Shaw slapped on the handcuffs and escorts White Boy to an officer. The officer shoves White Boy inside the patrol car and rushes to take him to booking. Shaw sat in his car debating on whether to help White Boy or not. Shaw knew that he can cover up the case making it look as if it was self-defense. He flipped his cell phone open and called on an old friend, Keith.

"Hello."

"Keith this is Detective Shaw, I have one of your little drug dealer's in custody."

"I see that you still have my number handy. You know that I don't hustle. I'm a businessman now. Haven't you heard? But who is this friend that's got himself into some trouble?"

Shaw laughed, "Isaiah, also known as White Boy. He is a murder suspect and other charges are pending. What would you like to do about this friend of ours?"

Keith knew then that the phone was safe to talk on but he still didn't want to take any chances. "What can we do to help our friend?"

"To help him, I'll need fifty thousand and the case will go away. I'll make the case be self-defense and he'll be a free man."

"Come by my new club and we'll talk. You just make sure that you do your job and you won't have to worry about our friend."

"The case will be closed just as fast as it opened. I'll take care of everything."

Less than an hour after booking, Keith sent his attorney to the jail bailing White Boy out in a hurry. The attorney informed White Boy that everything is taken care of and not to worry about the murder charge because it will be shown as self-defense. He'll get the judge to grant him probation for the weapon and reckless driving. White Boy thanked the lawyer for coming so soon and getting him off of a murder case. White Boy figures Reese acted soon he heard and sent the lawyer but the lawyer clarified that Keith sent him. After being released, Keith called.

"Thanks man for doing this for me. I really did fuck up."

"Don't worry about it. We're family. Just calm that hot shit out. You're drawing attention to your whole crew."

"Alright, I understand."

"I hear you gave the police a run for their money by not opening your mouth."

"I would never talk," White Boy said.

"I believe you. Tell Reese he owes me."

"I know that the lawyer cost you some money. I'll pay you back."

"Loyalty is all you have to pay." Keith said ending the call.

The lawyer took me home since my car is in the tow yard. Before turning the corner on his street, White Boy notices that his bedroom light is on. White Boy felt for his gun but Detective Shaw took it before he was taken to the county jail. White Boy feels naked. He didn't think Amad would be home because of what happened earlier. The lawyer noticed White Boy's nervousness and assured him that he don't have to worry. White Boy showed his toughness acting as if he's not worried about anything.

White Boy opened the door to total darkness. The only light on is in his bedroom.

Amad jumped out of the darkness.

"What up? How did you get out?" his voice trembles.

"Don't worry about how I got out. I like how you left me back there but you know what I'm not even mad. At least one of us got away."

"When I saw the police I panicked. I thought you would run too. I hid out at my cousin's house for a few hours before coming back home. Shit I just got here myself. I put everything back in your room. My fault man I didn't know what I was thinking."

White Boy walked inside his room being followed by Amad and checks the bag then begins to count the money. He sat aside the cocaine. It's less than the brick Amad was originally given. "Have you called anybody and told them what happened to us earlier?" White Boy asked sitting on his bed looking up at Amad.

"I didn't know what to say. I was worried about the police trying to find me."

"Don't worry about it; I'll call Reese soon as I finish counting and weighing the dope."

White Boy closed the door behind Amad and called Reese. Reese's phone goes to voicemail each time. White Boy left a message. After waiting for a few minutes, White Boy decided to call Tone.

Tone answered on the second ring with a groggy voice, "Damn man it's late as hell."

"My fault man for waking you but I need to talk to you."

"What's good?"

"Nothing is good. It is all bad," White Boy says sadly talking in a low tone.

Tone pulled the cover from over him and sit straight up in the bed. "What happened man? I know some shit was going to go down."

"Amad and I went over there to handle business, then some bitch came out shooting. I had to blast her."

"Oh shit!"

"The nigga got away while I was getting thrown in the back of a cruiser."

"You mean to tell me that he had left you and you went to jail? Where is he at now?" Tone questioned.

"He's here. He told me his side of the story and I understand why he left. Shit was crazy out there. He'd actually handle them niggas of his with me. I was shocked myself. He had got away with the shit we took and I have it all here so that is good."

"Fuck that shit. My nigga you are facing some time."

"It is a long story but Keith looked out with a lawyer for me. Guess what?"

"What?"

"Detective Shaw showed up on the scene. He even helped with the lawyer getting my charge to be self-defense. I have to go to court on the other charges but the lawyer said that I'll get probation so I'm not tripping."

"Damn nigga that's fucked up!"

"I'll be all right, it's a part of the game. I just wanted to tell you what happened. I tried to call Reese earlier but he isn't answering. I know I'll have to hear from him."

"I doubt it. He's going to be glad that you are out. I'll call either him or B in the morning. I have some good news for everybody. You and that scary ass nigga lay low. We'll meet up tomorrow."

"Did you call about that building?"

"That's the good news. Let me just say, Christian will be signing the paperwork tomorrow."

"Hell yeah. A'ight, I'll see you tomorrow," White Boy cheerfully said ending the call.

CHAPTER 6

REESE

I woke up this morning feeling great after another passionate night of lovemaking with Diana. All night I just looked at her and thought about our future together. After all these years of just being a couple, she is finally happy I made a serious commitment. When she's happy, I'm happy. As we made love last night, I caught her staring at the ring. Crazy as it sounds, when I was hitting her from the back and she was holding on to the headboard, I stared at the ring. I'm finally in love.

Minutes later, Diana brought me steak, scrambled eggs, buttermilk biscuits, orange juice, and a bowl of mixed fruit. I smiled from ear to ear as she hands me my plate. She must have gotten up early to be able to cook and comb her hair. Diana grabbed the bowl of fruit and feeds me a piece at a time. Diana suggested that we take a shower together. I told her we can but I want her now.

I pulled her closer to me allowing us to share kisses. Caressing her body and rubbing my hand over her silk robe. I untied the belt around her waist and slide her panties off. Gliding my hands up her thighs spreading them open for my fingers to be able to slip inside. I rolled my fingers over her clit to her liking, making her have an orgasm in no time.

Diana slid out the bed giving me a seductive look. I laughed as she teased me and walked into the bathroom. I slowly came up behind her. Diana stepped in first with the water hitting her body. The water flowed down her body as if she is standing under a waterfall. I lathered up her loofah and gently washed every inch of her body. When she was covered with bubbles, I gave her a soft massage soothing every muscle on her body. She pulled me closer and strokes my shaft. I picked her up wrapping her legs around my waist and with her back placed up against the wall I ease inside. She grabbed my neck and lets out a sensual moan. The water runs over top of us and her juice keep flowing. Diana begun to talk dirty, begging for me to stroke harder. I'd cuffed her legs up higher and position myself to dig deeper. The water turned cold giving me momentum to pound faster and harder. Her pussy became so wet and we come together.

Leaving out the bathroom, I'd gave her a hard slap on the ass showing her my satisfaction. We are both getting dressed in the bedroom but she was racing around the room putting clothes on while talking to the realtor. Watching her talk on her phone made me realize I haven't used nor seen my phone since last night. I hurried to put on a casual outfit and dress shoes before rushing downstairs to get my phone. I turned it on and already I have two messages. I also have a reminder telling me I have a business meeting today. Thinking for a second about the meeting and remember it's my date with Simone. Two days had passed since we met and I told her I wanted to get to know her better. I walked up a few stairs to see if Diana is ready to come down but she's still on the phone buying me some time to call Simone.

I'd tried calling Simone twice without receiving an answer. While I'm trying to call Simone, I'd received a text message. It's from B telling me to call him. I checked my voice messages. I have received a message from White Boy telling me he just got out of the County jail but thanks to Keith he got out. Feeling a little nervous, I needed to find out what happened. Tone also left a message saying he had spoken with White Boy and was going to look into the situation himself. He also mentioned that he and my brother would be meeting with the owner of the building to do the paperwork this afternoon.

Today will be yet another busy day. I had to take care of business before I can pleasure myself with Simone. With her on my mind I gave her another call.

"Hey lady, how are you?"

"I didn't think you were going to call."

"Why wouldn't I? I'm a man of my word. Remember you know how I conduct business."

"You are some shit. You really are living up to your reputation," Simone laughed.

"I'm just being me."

"Was that you trying to call me a few minutes ago?"

"Yes, I was calling to let you know I might be a little late for our date. I have some business to take care of first but I'll be there."

"I'm glad you called because I'm dealing with something with my girls. We also have some business to take care of. Just call me when you're done."

"That's a plan," I countered.

"Do I need to get myself all dolled up for you?" She asks playfully.

"You are already sexy as fuck. Just impress me."

"There you go again. I'll see you later and I want you to be ready. Now that I have your number, I'll text you my address," Simone said ending the call.

Rushing up the stairs, I saw Diana was finally dressed ready to go look at a house. I tried not to show a guilty look so I avoid eye contact. I put on my diamond earrings, watch, and brush my hair checking myself out in the mirror.

Diana eyes were all over me but I remained to give her eye contact while calling B. "Why are you putting your jewelry on just to go look at a house?" Diana questioned.

"I just feel like wearing it today. If we look like money they will treat us like money."

"You say some crazy stuff at times. Please hurry Reese, Ashley and B are on their way to look at the home next to us."

"I'm on the phone with B now."

"I'll be in the truck. Please don't take too long though. The realtor is also waiting for us." Diana says rushing outside.

"I'll be right out baby," I replied, spraying cologne over my body.

B chuckled hearing our conversation, "Man y'all arguing again?"

"No, we're all right. She's wondering why I'm getting fresh for today. You know I got a date."

"Man are you still going to kick it with Simone?"

"Yeah…! I reserved a suite for us down in Kentucky for the weekend. I'll pick her up after we get done doing business."

"Reese be careful with her man. Remember to wear a condom and don't let her near your phone. You don't need more problems with Diana."

"Let me worry about Diana. Trust me I'm taking a box down there."

"You'll need to take some protection. I'm talking about taking your 9mm."

"Good looking but I got this," I laughed.

"Man have you heard about what happened with White Boy and Amad?"

"Yeah…, I just checked my voicemail and heard the messages. I'm going to ask Keith what he thinks about the situation and if anything seemed weird."

"I've been on the phone all day. Tone wants us to meet up at the building that is for sale."

"That's good. Tone and Christian should have the paperwork complete by the time we get there."

"Yeah..., I called the jeweler and he said our jewelry is ready for us to pick it up."

"Damn that was fast. My shit better be right! We can go to the jeweler before we hook up with the boys."

Ashley interrupted our conversation. I could hear her rushing him to get off the phone to talk to the realtor. "Let me finish looking around so I can buy this house for her," B said.

"All right big money," I said joking.

"You have to see these homes. It's a nice neighborhood and everything is perfect. The house y'all are about to see is next door."

"I'm on my way now." I ended the call.

I finished putting on my jewelry and sprayed myself with some cologne. I wanted to look good and smell good. I added a designer jacket to match my outfit for a more professional look.

Entering the truck Diana sat on the passenger seat and keeps asking me why I'm dressed so nice. I'd ignored her ass and turn on a local radio station. She don't show much of an attitude but I can tell that she is wondering what I'm up to.

Knowing how impatient she is, I speed toward the house. We're greeted with a welcoming water fountain and a huge sign with the community's name. Driving through the neighborhood, we'd passed by a lake and a couple pushing a stroller in the unseasonably warm weather. I looked at Diana and I see in her face she's visualizing the couple as us. While we're riding, I studied each and every house. I never would have thought I would be living in a neighborhood like this.

Turning a few more corners, she finally points at the house we're to look at. Ashley's Lexus SC 430 is next door. Two empty lots separated us. The first thing I like is the wide driveway, and three-car garage. Stone steps lead us to the front door.

The realtor opened the door inviting us in. She walked us throughout the house and then the backyard. I was sold when I saw a half-court basketball area and enough yard for any kid to play. Diana loved the rain shower, granite countertops, vaulted ceilings, walk-in closets, and stainless- steel appliances. She signed the papers for the contract and came over to me with a huge smile. She told me she was finally happy. Her happiness cost us over $300,000. Now it was time for me to make some of the money back.

The realtor left us the keys and her contact information before leaving. Soon after, Ashley and B arrived. I busted out laughing from the worried look on B's face telling me he bought a house also. Ashley and Diana jingled their keys at each other with joy. Diana asked me to take her baby shopping wanting to buy paint for the baby room and other items but I had to let her down telling her that I had some business to do with the new connect. She was sad but tries to manage herself in front of our friends. I asked Ashley to take her back home so B and I could hit the highway. We didn't receive any lip walking out the door.

Driving off I called Keith and asked him about what happened last night with White Boy and Amad. Keith told me that White Boy and Amad were in a shootout and White Boy shot a girl. Amad got away with the money and dope while White Boy got caught trying to get away. Keith was able to send his lawyer down to the County jail and bail him out. He assured me that no one said a word and White Boy stayed true to himself and the crew. The lawyer and Shaw helped make the case looked as if it was self-defense to get White Boy off of murder charges. Keith didn't understand how Shaw arrived at the scene but Shaw did ask for fifty thousand for the help. I promised that I'll pay him back. I told him that I'll pay him as soon as possible but I'm preparing myself to escape the game. He understood completely and told me that I'll owe him a favor.

After talking to Keith a lot of shit was running through my mind. I knew I'd needed to get myself back focused in order for my team to be strong. We had too much to lose for my mind to be fucking up. I had driven all of the way to the jeweler without any memory of how I got there. The jeweler greeted us with a hug and a smile. He handed over B's ring and hung the necklace around my neck. We paid him and rushed out to meet with our boys.

CHAPTER 7

REESE

B and I opened the door entering the building that Tone had found for us. Christian was standing a few feet away with a stack of papers in his hand.

Amad caught my attention walking throughout the building and talking on his phone. He must had been talking to a female; he was acting all secretive and talking softly.

Christian and Tone walked toward us. Tone was carrying two bottles of vodka in each hand. White Boy slowly walked behind them holding his head down.

"Y'all see this? This is us. We own this. Can y'all believe it?" Tone said jumping up and down.

"Everything is finished and signed for?" I questioned believing that there is much more to buying a commercial site.

"Bruh, everything is done. I'll have some contractors fix up the place and we can be opening soon," Christian answered.

"I handled everything last night. I found a reasonable contractor to do the work inside of the club and pave a new parking lot. I also called Keith for his help to get us a liquor license. His lawyer joined us earlier to check the paperwork before Christian signed anything," Tone added.

"I read over each page carefully before I signed and everything is legit. The mortgage payments are not much considering how much we'll be bringing in each month. Tone gave the lawyer a hundred thousand dollars for the down payment although they only wanted fifty. We can have the building paid for within ten years or payoff the other four hundred thousand before the interest adds up," Christian said slowly.

"He's not worried about any money. Look at him and B, all shined up. I like that charm Reese," Tone said and grabs the chain for a closer look.

"I bought this today to impress Simone when I go to pick her up. I made some plans for us."

"You have to tell me how everything went when you get back," Tone smiled.

"Don't encourage him. I have already warned you about her. If it was me, I'd just fuck and keep it moving but I know you," B said.

"B I'm good. We're just going to get to know one another. You feel me?"

"Yeah right…"

"Come here White Boy. I need to talk to you man."

White Boy and I walked away. The others begun to drink and share ideas about the club. White Boy tells me that Amad asked him to go with him to collect the money or dope from the brick he had fronted his youngsters. White Boy says that everything was going as planned until some girl who he believes he knew came out shooting. Like I would've done, he shot back killing her instantly. Amad managed to escape while White Boy was being arrested.

What piqued my interest was that White Boy and Tone saw Shaw earlier and then he showed up on the scene to arrest White Boy. I see why Keith was so puzzled. I cut the conversation short and let him know that he did what was right and didn't have any choice but to shoot the girl. Although Keith helped him out of the situation, I assured him that it will soon pass.

We walked over to the boys and joined in the celebration. B and I decided it would be best for Amad to be done dealing dope and help Christian with the promotion of the club. Amad didn't like our decision and became furious. Amad stood up and shouted about us playing him. He pounded his fist in his palm. We all busted out in laughter from his actions. He took his seat and shook his head with anger.

B and I would take care of the employees, do the inventory, and make sure the building stay in good shape. White Boy and Tone will handle the security. Both of them like the sound of that.

Our first order of business will be getting the place cleaned up after the contractor's do their job. Christian announced that he in and his friends can start the cleaning today. I'd embraced Christian with a hug happy to see him taking on some responsibility.

Amad's phone rings. He quickly answers the phone and rapidly walks toward the door. He stands near the exit talking on his phone but turns his back not allowing us to hear.

"What's up with that muthafucka man?" Tone asked.

"I don't know but he has been acting like that lately," White Boy answered.

"For how long…?" I asked.

"Since he met some new bitch, that girl has his nose wide open. You know how some niggas act when they get some new pussy," White Boy said.

"That nigga got a bitch now!" Tone shouted.

"Some bitch from out of town. He hasn't brought her to the spot yet so he can't be fucking." White Boy laughed slapping hands with Tone.

"Fuck all of the jokes," I spat.

"I'll keep an eye on him," Tone replied.

"Good. Keep him close to you Tone," B said sternly.

Amad walked over. "Y'all I have to go do something. I'll get with y'all later."

White Boy grabbed Amad's shoulder. "I'll be at the house later. Tone and I are going back to Keith's strip club tonight."

"All right man. Try to relax and have some fun to get that shit off your mind. Christian are you ready to go yet?" Amad said.

"Yeah we can go. I have to go by the lawyer's office first before I drop you off." Christian responded walking toward the door.

"White Boy, y'all have fun. B and I will drive back down to buy some more work for the week."

"Oh yeah, Amad's boys from school check out. We can definitely do business with them. They're about their money." Tone interjected standing to his feet.

"Y'all still on that...? Christian, I'll be outside man. These niggas are tripping!" Amad aggressively responded screwing his face up.

"Alright we're gone. Tell Diana and my little nephew I said hi." Christian said, obviously trying to resolve the situation leaving out with Amad.

"Tone so these new niggas are ready to buy some work?" B asked turning to Tone.

"Yeah we can get them together whenever y'all ready. They want five bricks and didn't try to debate when I told them the price." Tone replied.

"Well y'all do what y'all need to do. We'll go grab the bricks from J and be back later. I'll link up with Simone after we drop the work off," I said.

"We won't be long at Keith's. I want to see if this girl is working there tonight. I'm going back to the house after that," White Boy says to me as B and I are walk out the door.

B and I drove over to get the money. B called J to place our order for fifteen bricks. J was surprise to hear from us so soon that he lowers the price. We're very glad because of the hefty down payment for the building.

We quickly drove to Cincinnati and back. I try to call White Boy and Tone but neither answers their phone. I assumed they're both still in the club being distracted by the women and music. I began to think about Simone and the things I wanted to do to her. Thinking about her sexy ass forces my foot to pressed on the gas.

Driving near our neighborhood I receive a call from Christian. The lawyer took a closer look at the paperwork and everything was great. I ask him where Amad is and Christian said he dropped him off about thirty minutes ago. With Amad's help with the dope I could leave fast.

Turning the corner I noticed a sports car driving away from the spot. I accelerate but they're already going too fast to chase. I parked in front of the house and constantly honk the horn hoping Amad is inside. He straggled out tugging at his baggy pants, talking on the phone. Amad didn't say a word to us opening the back door grabbing a duffel bag and walking back in the house and closing the door behind him.

B and I looked at each other knowing something's up. Grabbing the last bag we walked into the house. I'd threw my bag on the couch and a familiar scent crosses my nose. Looking around the room for a plug-in or some type of air freshener but none can be found.

Amad ended his phone conversation and I asked him about the scent. He looked at me crazy and ignored my question.

I stepped in the kitchen with B ready to breakout the dope and my phone starts vibrating. Simone sent me her address and a sexy comment saying she's ready to put it on me. I was excited to see what she's about. Quickly unzipping the bags dumping each brick on the table. B and I weighed each brick making sure each gram is accounted for. While we were measuring B nudged me toward Amad. He was acting real jittery with the dope.

"Amad are you all right?" I wondered staring him down.

"I'm still tripping about the shit that happened yesterday," Amad answered.

"Man let that shit go! Everything is under control. Shit, you got away," B said sternly.

"It's not that easy man. White Boy killed some innocent girl."

"You are acting like you killed her," I countered.

"Man she has people who care for her. Even if y'all get White Boy off someone is missing her."

"Nigga you worried about them bitch ass niggas who played you when they finally got their first brick!" B responded.

Amad sat on the couch silent shaking his head.

"Have you read the paper or watched the news today? Self-defense man, her people will hear those words." B tried to convince him.

"Reese you feel me don't you?" Amad asked.

"Man y'all did what y'all had to do. I have to go. Can y'all finish this up?" I said.

"Yeah we got this," B assured me waving me to leave.

I took four bricks to White Boy's room to store them and notice the safe is cracked open. I remembered closing it back after I grabbed some money for the dope. I took out all the money, count each dollar and we're short thousands of dollars. Who could have taken the money? All of us were at the building earlier. Suddenly the conversation I had with Christian cross my mind. He told me he dropped Amad off thirty minutes before we arrived. Amad never stole a dime before and his money was always right. Maybe I miscounted or we used the money on something that I couldn't recall. Shit maybe my mind was playing tricks on me.

Walking out of White Boy's room I hear Tone's speakers blasting. White Boy and Tone entered the house laughing and talking loud about their time at Keith's club. It's good to hear they had a good time. Now it's time for me to do the same.

"White Boy did you find what you were looking for?" I questioned.

"No. She wasn't there. Most of the girls didn't show today. I didn't know if it was because it was a little early but it was kind of empty. I did find someone else."

"Who…?"

"Peaches she came over to our table and sat down with us. Their other friend joined us also. I think her name is Cherish. Anyway, we shared some small talk just enough for me to get her number. Her friend wanted Tone but he wasn't interested."

"What!" B shouted.

"I'm cool on her. My girl is about something. She goes to school, do nails, and that chic ain't about shit," Tone defended himself.

I started for the door. "I'm about to find out what her friend is on."

"Hold up Reese, we'll walk out with you," Tone stopped me in my tracks.

"Amad give them five of them things," B ordered.

"Who do I look like?" Amad replied looking at B crazy biting down on his bottom lip.

B jumped up to trying to grab Amad but White Boy holds B back from attacking Amad. "I'll get the shit myself," White Boy said.

"Man keep on playing tough," B threatened pointing at Amad.

"You have been acting real funny. Nigga you need some pussy or something?" I teased Amad.

"Nigga I get pussy. Probably more than you," Amad said sarcastically.

Tone busted out with laughter.

"I bet. If you call your hand getting some pussy," I responded back.

"Whatever nigga," Amad said in a low tone.

"I do hear that you have a new chic so you might be getting a little but nothing close to how I get down. Was that her who had sped off before I had pulled up?" Tone asked.

"Hmm...no that was my cousin. I. I had left my gun over there and she was bringing it back," Amad stuttered.

"Amad, how about you ride with us to put your boys on? They're ready to meet up with us," Tone finally spoke up.

"Let me get my pistol."

"Why do you need that if these are your so called nigga?" Tone questioned.

"You never know."

"Damn right! Let's go," White Boy responded.

"Alright B I'll get at you when I get back," I said walking out.

I stepped outside with the rest of the crew but White Boy walks me to my truck. My thoughts are on Simone. I could see his lips moving but I'm not able to focus on his words although I did manage to hear that he was taking Peaches out tonight. White Boy always kept bad ass women around him but never seems to commit himself. Most of the women were attracted to him because of his wild ways, lavish spending, and he keeps himself in shape. I wondered why he went back to Keith's to find some girl when he has a phone full of numbers. I'd guess everything happens for a reason because he found Peaches. I regained myself and tell him to call me tomorrow so we can talk. I gave him a hug and jump inside the truck to call Simone.

CHAPTER 8

REESE

Speeding away from the spot heading in the direction of Simone's place, I played a nice R&B CD and mellow out. I noticed how the sun begins to set turning the sky into a reddish orange color. Not wanting her to think I forgot about our date, I decided to call before popping up on her.

"Simone this is Reese, what's up?"

"I know it's you boy," Simone said playfully.

"I haven't forgotten about you. I'm on my way now and would like for you to pack some clothes for the entire weekend."

"The whole weekend…? You really want to spend some time together," she sounds surprised.

"I made some reservations for a room down in Kentucky. Take your time I still need to make a stop at the gas station to get a fill up and wash this muthafucka. Are you still handling business with your girls?"

"No. We're done. You just get your fine ass here." Simone turns away from the phone to say something. "I'm so sorry about that. That's my girl Peaches acting silly because she's going on a date tonight with your boy."

"Yeah he mentioned it to me. He's excited. I'll be at your house soon as I leave the gas station," I said ending the call.

Arriving at the gas station, I filled the truck up and take it through the automatic washer. I'd left the gas station feeling and smelling good. I can't wait to see Simone so I speed to her condo taking the highway route.

As I removed the keys from the ignition, I saw Cherish opening the door for Peaches. Peaches rushed out the house but slows her pace walking down the steps. I watched her breasts bounce with each step. She was dressed very nicely, with a pair of heels on, a sexy fitted shirt, and stretchy pants which revealed her luscious curves answering why her name was Peaches. I closed my door.

She caught me looking at her. "Boy you better stop before Simone comes out here tripping believing that I'm trying to take her man."

"She ain't on that. Besides you do look nice."

"Thank you but that is my girl and she likes you a lot. It was nice seeing you again but I have a date with White Boy." Peaches waves goodbye, cheerfully walking to her Mercedes CL 350.

I walked up to the door only ringing the doorbell once and Simone opens the door instantly. Thinking about B's warning I placed my hands inside my jacket and grip the gun handle. I always warn my boys of situations like this and now I was in the situation.

Simone greeted me with a smile and opens her arms for a hug. Looking better than she did when I first seen her. Once again her nails and hair is done. She wore a light brown blouse that complements her hazel eyes and a pair of sandy brown heels to match. Her blue spandex pants show the thickness of her thighs and her blouse revealed just enough cleavage to remain classy. Simone's breasts aren't as big as Diana's but look damn good on her body.

 Hugging her, pulling her body closer to mine, we stare into each other's eyes and she lets out a small giggle. I take her hands and place them on my shoulders. I study the curve of her lips shaped into a perfect letter "M". Her lips are full and glazed with gloss. We exchanged kisses. The taste of sweet watermelon is on my tongue.

Cherish interrupted us acting as if she is clearing her throat. We laugh and enter the house together. Simone breaks away from me to whisper softly to Cherish. I lick my lips with thoughts of tasting her cross my mind. She turned her head looking back at me and noticed how I was checking her out.

"Damn you look good."

"I taste good to if that is something you would like to find out," she said.

"I might have to see about that." I countered.

Simone steps in front of me allowing me to get a closer look at each and every curve. "Boy don't tease me if you're not up to the challenge."

"I don't have any reason to tease you," Sitting down on the couch I have a perfect view of her fat pussy.

"I hear you. Wait right here so I can finish getting my things."

Simone walked back to what I assumed was her bedroom. Cherish and I began to share a conversation about my plans with Simone but Simone yell for her assistance leaving me alone. I looked around her house and noticed that everything was new. The loveseat I was resting on still had that new leather smell. Strangely there wasn't a television anywhere in sight. This place cost some cash.

Simone exit the bedroom looking like she'd just stepped out of an urban magazine. I liked how she coordinated a diamond charm bracelet to match a diamond necklace with a diamond pendent resting in between her breasts. Now her cleavage was more intriguing. Simone knew what she was doing and I had to admit she was doing it well. I believed Keith's right about her. She was out here doing something and was getting paid very well. Tonight was my night to find out as much about her as I can.

I take her suitcases and follow behind her walking out of the house. Simone takes her time stepping down each step and I watch her ass jiggle. I sit her suitcases in front of the truck and see the reflection of my gun in the front grill. I look up to make sure she doesn't notice but I was too late. She smiled and walked over to the passenger door waiting for me to open it. I placed the suitcases in the trunk and laughed. The only women I opened doors for was my mother and Diana. But not wanting to destroy the mood, I opened the door and help her inside.

I climbed inside the truck. She reclined her seat and stared at me with a curious look. Figuring that she might be wondering why I was carrying my gun or she might be scared of guns. I placed the gun away inside of the glove compartment to help her feel more secure. Simone remained still until I turned the ignition and the music played through the speakers. She jumped up from her seat and sang along with the lyrics. I would not have thought that she would like to ride to R&B music mixed with Ohio's classic bands.

We didn't talk much for the first thirty minutes of our trip, we just shared some small talk about songs. I sped through the traffic weaving in and out. We crossed the bridge entering Kentucky. Fifteen minutes before arriving at the theme resort Simone turned down the music. I looked over at her with a surprising expression.

She placed her hand on my thigh.

"Why did you decide to take me down here?" Simone asked staring in my eyes.

"I want to spend some alone time with you. To get to know you better like I had said before. You know a lot about me but I don't know much about you," I answered.

"When I first heard about you, I wanted to meet you."

"You heard a lot."

"You act like people don't know who you and your boys are. Everybody knows who Reese is. I heard about you from my friend and it was too good to be true." Simone rubbed her hand over my thigh.

"That's gossip that's all. Besides I don't do shit for anyone to want to know me."

"You don't do shit but you are walking around here with a gun. Come on I know better. I have cousins who have been dealing for years. I know a nigga who's hustling."

"Hustling is what it is. It might sound good to you and others but this shit ain't what's up. I'm getting out of the business soon. We have a real business that is legit now."

"What kind of legitimate business are you all getting into to keep from selling dope?"

"We just bought a club. You and your friends are more than welcome to come when we open."

"We will."

"That reminds me. You and your friends going through something…?"

"Why are you asking that?" she questions with a confused look.

"When I called earlier you said y'all were having some issues and had to take care of business. Then, this whole trip you've been quiet and distant like something is on your mind."

Simone wiped her face trying to hold back her tears. "Yes, we're dealing with something but we'll handle the situation. I'm glad to get away for the weekend. You can help me release some stress."

"You don't have to worry about that."

"I'm sure I won't."

"What kind of business are you and your friends in to?"

Simone placed her finger over my lips and whispers for me to be quiet. Taking her finger away she placed soft kisses along my neck. She took my words away even though I had so much to ask her. Simone skillfully and gently unbuckled my pants. She pulled out my dick and stroked it firmly causing me to stiffen quickly. Simone confidently takes my shaft and places it in her mouth. She swirled her tongue over the head causing me to veer in the next lane. She didn't frighten but continues to bounce her head up and down.

"Hold on wait a minute. We're getting off on the next exit," I said trying to resist the pleasure.

"I told you to be ready for me," Simone teased applying lip gloss back on her lips.

"I see. Wait until I get your ass in the room."

After receiving the key cards to our room, I grabbed our luggage and take them inside. We walk around the room checking it out. She falls in love with the Jacuzzi but instantly gets upset when she remembers she didn't pack a swimsuit. I'd joked around and playfully tell her she doesn't need one. She bashfully smiled and teased me by pulling down her pants showing me her ass. I unzipped my bag and pulled out a bottle of champagne. Pouring us two glasses I noticed she has stripped to her thong panties. Opening the blinds in the moonlight, she stroke a pose showing all of her goodies. I'd asked her to come closer to me so that I can caress her body. Simone walked toward me like a runway model, the sound of her heels echoed throughout the room. The way she was swaying her hips from side to side reminds me of an old school balance beam. Her thong hugs her hips as if begging me to pull it off.

"Are you going to get in with me or are you going to stand there looking?" Simone asks with a sad face pointing to the Jacuzzi.

I'd thought about doing both because either way I can't lose. "Hmm…"

"Reese stop playing with me," she said pushing my arm.

"Yeah I'll get in with you. Why don't you take these glasses over with you to the tub and I'll get us some towels."

"Don't take too long. I get bored real easy."

I watched her walk toward the tub. I studied her ass and imagine myself behind her slapping her ass giving her pain and pleasure. Her ass looked good in pants and a dress, and now naked it was phenomenal. Simone teases me and slowly bends over to place the glasses. She looked over with a seductive smile. Cautiously she placed one leg in at a time. Finally, she sat down under the bubbles and requested I get in, yet again.

I'd hurried to the bathroom. I'd stripped to my boxers and check myself in the mirror. Quickly, I dropped to the floor and knockout fifty push-ups to give myself a quick blow to show off my muscles. Dusting my hands off, I heard Simone yelling for me to come on. I grabbed the towels and robes rushing into the living room.

I'd dimmed the lights after closing the blinds setting the mood just right. Setting the towels and robes aside on the floor, Simone looked at me with intriguing eyes. I look back at her noticing she has taken her hair down. She compliments my body and stood up to feel my chest.

Sitting next to her, we converse for thirty minutes straight. We talked about our friends, my interest with going legit, and about us. It was weird how much we'd had in common. She was opened to discussing my relationship with Diana and wanted to know where Diana and I are in our relationship. Simone understands Diana was my world but she wanted to be a part of it also. She told me about her past relationships with other men who were dealing and that she'd also has a thing for women. I'm not surprised knowing that most bisexual women are super freaks. She laughed when I told her that I'm cool with having a woman who is bisexual. Simone and I understood each other very well.

"Whenever you are not busy with your woman and your business, I would like to be with you," Simone said meaningfully.

I lightened up the atmosphere and tell her a few jokes. We laugh and playfully splash each other with water. Simone plays like I had splashed her in the eye so I tried to apologize and she sneaks a kiss. She sat on my lap while we exchanged passionate kisses as my shaft rapidly gets erect. I pulled her hair back and take my time kissing her neck down to her breast. I suck on her brown nipples and rub her clit. She tried to resist taking my head and placing wet kisses on my lips.

After a few strokes, she stepped out the tub and slowly takes off her thong like a striper at Keith's club. The bubbles slid down her sexy body. She was dripping wet. Her hair laid across her nipples begging for me to lift each of them into my mouth. Simone bent over for the towel allowing me to see her pussy from the back. I grabbed myself and stroke at the sight. She reached down to help me out of the tub but I took her hand and place her ring finger in my mouth. I stepped out and smoothly rub my hands over her body.

She playfully pushed me away tucking the towel under her breasts. We both took a glass and walk toward the bedroom holding hands.

We stopped directly at the foot of the bed. She shoves me down onto the bed and quickly drops to her knees placing all of me in her mouth. Simone stroked and sucked my erect shaft slowly popping it out of her mouth and back in again. I laid back with my eyes closed enjoying the sensation. She climbed on top of me and bounces and rolls her ass with perfect rhythm. I grabbed hold of her ass, taking control and forcing her ass down my shaft. She slaps my hands away and pushed me back down to take back control.

Suddenly she hopped up and goes through her suitcase. Simone told me that she is going to take a hot shower and prepare herself for me. She claimed that tonight will be a night that I would be happy with her and not Diana.

Soon as Simone entered the bathroom, I jumped to my feet and run into the living room to do some snooping.

I'd hastily shuffled through her purse, careful to make sure everything remains intact. Nothing seems out of the ordinary all I find is regular women hygiene and beauty products. I pull out a small address book. Flipping through it, I'd noticed all the names are men from different cities and one woman with a kiss print next to it. The past is the past I told myself. When I put the book back in its place, I heard the shower cut off. I quickly zip the purse but notice another zipper. I didn't want to get caught but I have a feeling that she isn't telling me everything about her. I unzipped it and find her credit cards and multiple identification cards from Michigan, Ohio, and New York.

"Reese where are you?" Simone called from the bathroom.

"I haven't left you. I had to check my phone and grab the bottle for us."

"You better not have left me. Come back here I have something for you."

I sat on the edge of the bed anticipating for her to enter the bedroom. Begging to think deeply about what I had found in her purse, drinking directly from the bottle taking deep gulps. Since Simone is taking her time to come out, I decided to text Diana and let her know I was all right. I started to text and Simone walked out with sexy lingerie on. I sent the message without taking my eyes off her. Taking another gulp and maintaining eye contact.

Simone stood at a side profile and shine her ass with oil adding more sex appeal. She took the bottle from me and drinks a sip herself before setting it aside. Placing her foot between my thighs she asked for me to oil her legs and I didn't hesitate to do it. I massaged her legs gently rubbing the oil into her skin.

Simone took off the lingerie giving me a strip tease. She skillfully placed a condom in her mouth and slides it on me. I stood up picking her up into my arms and she rode the fuck out of my dick. Holding onto her pillow soft ass tightly forcefully thrusting inside her wet pussy, feeling her juices drip down my shaft I took her to the bed and dig inside her.

Resisting myself from having an orgasms I pulled out to taste her pussy. Simone goes crazy squirming over the covers. I get her pussy so wet her juices not only are on the sheets but covers my mouth. Not letting her rest I quickly flip her over into doggy-style and slide back inside her. Simone bounces her ass on me rapidly. I reached around her grabbing her breasts with both hands giving myself deeper penetration. Simone begs for me to allow her to take control but I continued to thrust. When I heard her scream, my body gives in and released a powerful orgasm.

We went back and forth all night until the morning sun rose. She rested her head on my chest and we fall asleep.

Saturday morning came and gone. We woke up in the afternoon and have sex soon as our eyes open. Simone let me fuck her in all types of positions and even allows me to record her sucking my dick. Simone wore me out today making me ask for a break. After hours of sex, we'd ordered in some dinner and watch a romantic movie. Then, we had sex for the rest of the night.

Today was our last day here so I took her to a nice restaurant to observe the views of Kentucky and the Cincinnati area. We walk along the Ohio River. While we were trying to talk, our cell phones rung. Tone called to ask how good her pussy is, which I couldn't answer because she was standing right next to me. White Boy was trying to talk to me about some drama that he and Peaches had but Simone and I were back in the room packing. I was still on the phone with him when she gives me a last suck goodbye. Simone and I briefly talked about how we're going to go about our relationship. I wanted to keep our relationship confidential. If Diana finds out, our plans will be over and I was not having it. Simone only asks that I stay away from other bitches besides Diana and that I let her know when I was leaving town. Simone didn't want to miss out on some good dick when I find the time.

CHAPTER 9

WHITE BOY

I tried to talk to Reese before he left to be with Simone but he wasn't paying me any attention. We talked about Peaches but I really wanted to tell him about the images popping in my head. Every time I close my eyes I see the girl I shot. I think something was trying to tell me that I knew her.

I'd went through so many girls I didn't remember their names but lately I haven't been with a new bitch or fucked any. Besides Cincinnati, the only other place I'd been to see some bitches was at Keith's club. The night we went there I got so drunk I could hardly remember shit.

I asked Tone to ride back to Keith's to see if I could recognize anybody working there. I didn't recognize anybody in the club so we leave. The whole situation was driving me crazy and the only one I thought would listen was Reese.

We all are like family but I looked up to Reese like a big brother. He stopped me from doing stupid shit and kept my head straight. I believed he wasn't paying me any attention because I let him down and the team. I'd have to prove my worth again.

Tone drove us over to Lamar's house. Since the police confiscated my gun I had to get another one fast. Lamar better known as Mar, and Scotty sold dope but they had a connect for guns for a very low price. Mar showed me all types of automatic weapons, semi-automatic weapons, shotguns, and a bullet proof vest. I bought a .40 caliber handgun and hurried out in order to handle business.

We met with Amad's new crew. The Five Oaks area was surrounded by run down homes, abandoned apartments, prostitution, and drugs. Besides our meeting spot, they couldn't have chosen a better place.

People might knew what was going on but they would keep their mouth shut.

Tone watched me while he conducted the transaction. Amad acted nervous as hell fidgeting. He might be acting this way because he didn't get a chance to do the dirty work.

The two guys we met before greeted us with three others armed with automatic machine guns. I pulled my shit out. Stepping behind Tone I'd watched his back. The two main guys talked with an east coast slang. Amad stood quietly next to me. He didn't say much to any of them besides saying "What's up" when we first arrived. Tone exchanged the dope and passed the bag of money to Amad. Tone ordered Amad to count the money before we left and he walked back to the truck. Minutes later, Amad rolled down the window shouting that the money was correct. Tone shook their hands and we pulled off happily.

We returned to the house. Tone paid me my cut receiving a lot of attitude from Amad. He threw his hands in the air and frowned his face. Amad thought he should've gotten a cut also. He claimed he deserved more than me because he put everything together. I laughed at his stupid ass and go to my room. I heard Amad continuing the argument but Tone ignored him.

I'd quickly get dressed and then called Peaches. This woman didn't believe I still wanted to take her out when I explained that my car was in the tow yard. She thought I was trying to lie my way out of our date but I assured her I wanted to see her badly. I told her I would like to take her to a casino and hotel and out to a club down in Cincinnati to see how good she could work her ass. Finally she agreed to drive so I gave her the directions to my house and waited for her arrival.

I stood in the front window looking out of the blinds every few minutes, the door- bell rung and caught me off guard. I tucked my gun inside my waistband and slowly opened the door. Peaches stood at the door with her designer shades on looking sexy as fuck. I wanted to skip all the bullshit and take her back to my bedroom to blow her back out.

I slid into her new Mercedes and instantly fired up my exotic weed. Peaches looked at me with a strange expression. I blow out a cloud of smoke and she snatched the blunt from my hand and began to smoke like a champ herself. I become comfortable and we passed the blunt back and forth listening to some reggae music.

She sped to the casino, sometimes doing up to one hundred miles an hour. I gave her five hundred dollars to play on some tables but she'd played the slot machines. Taking the stack of cash Tone gave me and play on the black jack table. I lose five hundred quickly but Peaches encouraged me to continue. My next hand, I won my money back. Peaches gave me a tight hug. I bet big and win three hands in a row. I shouted with excitement attracting a crowd to my table. I'd bet higher not caring about if I won or lost. Peaches became jealous smacking her lips and walking away toward the bar. Although she left me, I look over in her direction ever so often. I won four more hands before leaving the table with my chips.

I'd cashed in my winnings and we left the casino. Peaches drove with a blank look on her face staring out the windshield. I wanted to ask her what was on her mind but I remained silent.

We arrived at the club just in time before the crowd really show. She hesitated to get out the car knowing how popular the club was. I assured her I just wanted to take her in to have a good time. Peaches begged for me not to be in long and tried to persuade me to go to a boring restaurant. I'd practically dragged her into the club.

When we entered the club, I'd walked her straight over to an empty table. I asked a waitress for a bottle of champagne. Peaches nervously looked around the club. I asked her what was on her mind and she told me she didn't like the atmosphere. I didn't understand because the club was mellow and far from ghetto.

The club DJ played a new R&B hit. Peaches begun to dance in her seat. I asked her if she would like to dance. She hesitated but said yes. Like a gentleman, I took her by the hand and escorted her to the dance floor with the other couples. Peaches seductively grinded on me and allowed me to feel on her soft body. We danced four straight songs. When the DJ changed the mood playing an upbeat song we took our seats. We drunk sharing conversation and I humor her with my silliness. Peaches finally felt comfortable with me and took a seat on my lap dancing again. I interrupted her and walked off to the restroom.

Inside the restroom some nigga asked if I would mind if Peaches would dance with him. I told him it is up to her and that she isn't my woman. He quickly changes his attitude and tells me that he knows her. He claims Peaches use to fuck with his brother about two years ago. He warns me to watch her because she set his brother up to be robbed.

Leaving the restroom I'm confused. I walked back over to the table and sat across from her. Peaches continued to dance in her seat waving her hands and drink in the air. The waitress came back asking if we needed anything else and I told her I would like two shots of vodka. The waitress came back quickly, sitting down the glasses. I tipped the waitress and I gave her a friendly smile. Peaches snapped about the gesture. I downed the next glass screwing my face up at her. She'd apologizes for getting upset and wondered what was up with me noticing my empty glasses. I ignored her, pissing her off. She hopped up and told me that she wanted to leave. I told her to leave and drink the rest of the champagne. Peaches stomped away, leaving me at the table alone. She didn't leave the club but found herself a table near the exit. I watched her carefully from across the room. Niggas and bitches were rejected by her as soon as they stepped to her. A few of those bitches I would love to fuck. Peaches pulled out her phone from her purse and proceeded to talk, probably bad talking me to her friends. Feeling the liquor rushing through my body, I got up to use the restroom yet again.

Coming out of the restroom I could hear an argument over the music. The only two security guards rushed over to the commotion. I took my seat and tried to find Peaches but she was nowhere in sight. I'd downed the rest of the champagne directly from the bottle. I heard a woman's voice cry out. I stood looking in the direction of the woman's voice. Surprisingly it was Peaches shouting at the guards to stop touching her. I'd rapidly walking over to her pushing people out of the way, I slide in between the guard and grabbed Peaches by the wrists, trying to steer her away from the guards but she kept talking shit.

Behind me was the guy from the restroom shouting at Peaches calling her out of her name. He warned me about her again. Peaches took a drink from a nearby table and throws the glass at him ruining his shirt. He pushed the other guard off of him and tried to hit Peaches but hits me on the cheek. I'd let go of her wrist and quickly hit him two times in the face dropping him to the floor. His partner tried to tussle with me but the guards separate us and push me toward the exit.

Peaches was furious and asked me to drive because her nerves were bothering her. I hoped in the driver seat and checked my face out in the mirror making sure I did not have a bruise. I thought about his warnings. I wondered if anything he said was true.

Peaches slammed her purse on the dashboard. She denied setting his brother up but confessed that she did take some money and jewelry from him. She claimed that when they were together he used to beat her so she took what she was owed. I understood completely.

I'd begun to roll back in reverse but a car blocks me. The nigga I knocked out rapidly jumped out his car heading our way. I didn't have time to reach under the passenger seat. Peaches pulled out a small pistol from her purse. She quickly shifted in her seat and aimed directly at him. When he gotten to the back bumper he stops in his tracks staring down Peaches. Peaches ordered for him to tell his friend to move the car or he'll get shot. He complied. Sternly she told him to put down his gun and kick it aside. When his friend moves the car, I pressed down on the gas flying out the parking lot.

CHAPTER 10

REESE

After taking Simone home, I drove over to the spot. Tone's truck and Christian's car are parked in the driveway. White Boy's car must still be towed. I hope he was here because I want to finish the conversation we were having before I left with Simone.

I walked in to overhear Tone, B and Christian discussing the club. Christian has the contractors at work already. The club will be ready within a month. I headed over to them and slap their hands. They told me what's been done to the club already and I'm very impressed.

I asked Tone about the meeting with Amad's new crew. He said that the money was in the back and they will need more soon. I'd took the bag of money from White Boy's room and throw it down on the kitchen table. While I count, I wondered where Amad and White Boy are. I placed a few stacks aside and called White Boy but he didn't answer. I looked over toward B and Tone asking them about White Boy. Tone told me that Amad and White Boy went to get White Boy's car out of tow. I shrugged my shoulders and start to count again.

Diana stopped my count by texting me to hurry so we can buy some things for the house and for the baby. I'd rapidly finished counting the money and quickly walked to White Boy's room throwing the bag inside of his closet. The boy's question why I'm in such a hurry I assure them that I'm okay but I have to get home. Explaining myself to them I received message after message from Diana rushing me to get home.

Pulling up to the house Diana was standing in the driveway with her bag on her shoulder, hand on hip. Her facial expression was warning me not to get her mad. Although I had only been gone for the weekend I noticed the baby has grown inside her. I looked at her with a smile on my face, happy to have her in my life. I cannot imagine my life without her and I was taking the steps for us to have a better life.

We pulled out the driveway and my phone constantly chimes. I ignore the text messages. Diana stares me up and down every time my phone chimes. She looks at me, waiting for me to answer or to text back. I finally play along with her game and check the messages; they are from Simone talking nasty. Diana tries to read my face while I'm reading each message but I kept a straight face. I'd put my phone back down. Diana resisted my eye contact and conversations. She took out some newspaper advertisements and reads through them. I'd read the advertisement and drive to that store without her giving me any direction.

We go to an expensive furniture store and buy furniture for the house having it delivered to us. Then, we shopped for the baby. We registered some baby items but it seem as if I bought everything. Diana enjoyed shopping for the baby, sharing her excitement with me. When we were in line to pay for the items, White Boy called me. He told me he and Amad went to the same jeweler and bought him a diamond chain. He got a ring made with the emblem. Diana signal for me to get off the phone so I could pay the cashier. I told White Boy I would try to call him later but he told me to come back over to the spot so I could see his new twenty-eight inch rims. I asked him how was he able to be doing all of the shopping and he told me that he hit a lick over the weekend. White Boy tried to assure me he didn't do a lot of spending like I thought he does. He claimed he had bought all of this to go back up to Keith's to show off. White Boy told me he had to go back up there because he believed the girl he shot worked there. He confessed to me he had been unable to sleep because she stayed in his dreams. The stress had taking a toll on him causing him to drink and smoke more often. I paid the cashier and walked away continuing my conversation. Walking into the parking lot, I tried to recommend that he cleared his mind and maybe spend some time with Peaches. I opened the door for Diana and ended my call with White Boy, tossing my phone on the seat. As I load the truck, I think the shooting was driving White Boy crazy.

I decided to call B but my phone wasn't on the seat. Diana tossed the phone in my lap and stared out the passenger window. I wondered if she went through my phone and read the flirtatious messages from Simone.

The whole way home Diana didn't say a word to me. She was on the phone with one of her girlfriends talking bad about niggas in general but I knew that her words are for me. Diana quickly jumped out the car and rushed inside the house slamming the door behind her. I brought the baby items inside and asked her to wait for me in the bedroom. She rolled her eyes but complies anyway. I made her a bubble bath and light some candles. I took her bathrobe to her and ask her to get undress. While she relaxed inside of the tub, I hurried and cook us dinner.

Diana walked into the kitchen seeing the table set with the food ready for us to eat. She tried not to cry wiping her face. I'd laughed at her happiness and pulled out a chair for her. We sat down and enjoyed dinner together. After we ate, we sat on the couch and watched a reality show together. We both are enjoying the show and each other's company until my phone vibrated on the kitchen counter. Diana rushed over to the kitchen. I'd tried to grab her but she slipped out of my grasp. She answers the phone with an attitude yelling into the phone talking shit.

"Why are you calling my man? Hello. Now you can't talk you stupid ass bitch!"

Then she threw the phone against the wall. I'd walked over to console her but the closer I got she warned me to get away.

"Reese please get away from me. I didn't want you touching me right now." Diana said turning away from me. Reaching my arms out to embrace her she pushed my arms away and she run to the bedroom and slammed the door so hard the pictures bounced on the wall. I waited to run in behind her so I could see what got her so upset. Simone had tried to call me and quickly hung up hearing Diana's voice. I'd became so upset I threw the phone down.

I'd tried to turn the knob but it was locked. I'd tapped on the door just loud enough for her to hear me but I didn't receive any response. I placed my ear on the door and I heard her talking shit to someone about the situation. I'd banged on the door like a mad man.

"What do you want?" she yell.

"I want you! I know I fucked up."

"Damn right you did. I'm tired of these games you are playing. I'm tired of hearing your name in bitches' mouths when I finally go out and now I have to come home to it."

"What are you talking about?"

"When I went to go get my hair and nails done, some bitches came in talking about you and your boys."

"So! Fuck them bitches! Bitches are going to talk," I spat punching the door.

Diana cried, "I was embarrassed. I'm sitting here relaxing and some ghetto ass bitches are talking about my man. The bitches were running their mouth about how y'all were spending money on them and acting like monkeys."

"That's how bitches talk."

"No, Reese! What really pissed me off was when they were jealous because you didn't fuck with them but went to talk to some other bitch."

I'd braced myself up against the door and stand silent.

"I wanted to trust you but after hearing them I had no choice. Reese I saw the messages from her. I guess she's the bitch those girls were talking about. Are you going to tell me about her?"

"Diana please open the door. I don't want to keep talking through the door."

The door slowly opened. Diana walked back to the bed.

"Don't stop talking now," she ordered.

"The girl is nobody. I did meet her at the club. She wanted to talk business and that was it. Trust me you do not have to worry about her. I'm focused on you and the baby," I'd scooted next to her.

"I know I don't have anything to worry about because the next time I hear about her I'm gone." Diana's eyes filled with tears.

I'd hugged her tightly burying her face into my chest and whispered promises in her ear.

CHAPTER 11

REESE

A month had passed since we had bought the house. We'd been living in the house and enjoying each day together. Diana had decorated the house beautifully. I'd bought all of the expensive furniture she liked since we're still connected to James but our club will open tonight.

Christian oversaw all of the maintenance work and with Tone's help, hired the staff. The only time Christian needed anyone's input was when he needed to buy furniture, items for the bars, lighting, audio systems, and suggestions for the name of the club. I really saw the leadership qualities Christian had in him. Having yet to see the finishing touches on the club, so tonight will be a surprise. Christian asked if I would ask the crew to spend some extra money on hiring two famous R&B singers to perform tonight. He assured me we'll get our money back plus some by adding them to the headliner. I agreed and Christian did all of the promotions expecting a large crowd.

Last night I could barely sleep with the excitement about the club and spent some of the night with Simone. I came home and didn't try to sneak in the bed because I didn't want to disturb Diana. However, I did manage to get inside the bedroom and place a necklace next to her on the nightstand for a surprise Valentine's gift. I crept out the room and down the stairs so I could get some sleep.

It was hard to get myself comfortable on the couch but as soon as I closed my eyes I fell asleep. Maybe not even ten minutes had passed when my phone rung. I pulled out the phone turning it off before Diana heard the ringing and come down tripping. Earlier in the day I was going to take Diana some flowers and the flight tickets to work but I got caught up with Simone. I placed the tickets and my phone on the coffee-table. I instantly fell back to sleep.

Diana's soft touch woke me. I kept my eyes closed and enjoy her slowly undressing me. She struggled to pull off my boxers so I turned on my side helping her get them off. I peeked to see what she was doing next. Diana folded my clothes neatly placing them on the loveseat. I watched her cautiously admiring her ass. She turned back to me and caught me looking. Without hesitation she dropped her robe to reveal her red and black lingerie. Diana touched herself and took her wet finger inside her mouth. She climbed on top of me with her breasts in my face slowly slid down my chest.

"Good morning," she whispered.

We exchanged kisses instantly arousing me. Diana feed me fresh strawberries and rubbed flavored oil over her breast and ass.

I tried to sit up to get a taste but she pushed me back. I laid back closing my eyes and allowed her to make good love to me. Within minutes I fell back to sleep satisfied with a powerful orgasm.

The afternoon sun peeked through the blinds waking me up. I gently took Diana's arm from my chest and quickly got dressed so I could work out. I turned on my phone and it begun to vibrate. I had a reminder set telling me to pick up my suit from the cleaners for tonight's opening. I had so much to do but with so little time.

"Reese what would you like for me to cook for breakfast?" Diana woke up asking.

"Baby I can't sit around today. I have some business to handle early."

She'd became upset stumping away rushing downstairs into the kitchen. I heard her making some smoothies while I laced my shoes. I got ready to exit the house and she stopped me with a tall glass of a fruit smoothie. She insisted I drink it before leaving.

A few minutes later, I'm driving to the gym. I called Tone and B on a conference call. They both were excited about tonight and wanted me to meet them at the club now but I tell them that I would not be able to be there until later. B knew that my night with Simone had me running behind and told me that he would see me later.

Simone and I had not been seeing each other as much as she would like because I had been trying to do right by Diana. I found myself spending any extra free time with Simone addicted to her physically. Since we mostly got together late at night, all we ended up doing was fucking. She went out of her way doing something new in the bedroom and tried to find a way to keep me there with her. Simone told me her feelings are getting real with me but I had not allowed myself to get too close with her. There still was a mystery about her.

I went to the house and begin undressing. I heard Diana somewhere in the house talking on her phone. I went into the bathroom and after showering I decided to take the clippers over my hairline and face for a clean look.

I rushed out the shower barely having my towel wrapped around me knowing I have to still get my suit. I quickly dried off putting on my boxers and socks when I noticed my suit lying across the bed still inside the plastic from the cleaners, next to a pair of new and perfectly matching loafers. Diana must have had the cleaners deliver it. I dressed myself in the mirror looking at myself very closely.

Diana walked up behind me sliding her arms through mine.

"What's up are you going to get dressed?" I asked.

"You know I don't like going to clubs. Ashley and I are going to let you and B celebrate as men together without us women. She's coming over to chill out with me."

I turned around to hug her. "Thank you baby, it's probably best that you didn't come because of the crowd and we can't risk something happening to you or my son."

"You just know the baby's a boy. We'll find out soon." Diana laughed.

Diana gave me a soft kiss and tightens my tie. We were interrupted by the doorbell. We walked together and open the door for Ashley. Ashley and Diana hugged and talk about the baby. I heard Ashley complimenting the necklace I bought for Diana as I walked over to the coffee table to pick up the envelope with our airfare tickets and hotel information.

Ashley and Diana sat down on the couch, still talking. I grabbed my keys and cell phone and start for the door.

Diana hopped up to her feet stopping me at the door.

"You were not going to leave without giving me a kiss were you?"

"No," I kissed her.

"That is how y'all made the baby," Ashley playfully interrupted.

We laughed separating.

"I'll be home early tonight," I promised.

"Have a good time with your friends and enjoy yourself. Thank you for this beautiful necklace. It is real pretty. Did you like your gift this morning?" She stared into my eyes.

"Every minute and guess what?"

"What baby?" She straighten my jacket.

"I have one more gift for you," I smiled as I hand her the envelope.

Diana opened it and shouts with excitement. "Oh baby thank you!"

"What is in the envelope girl?" Ashley asked Diana repeatedly. Diana can't answer. Tears rolled down her face.

I gave her one more kiss before leaving for the club.

Slowly I drove behind a line of cars I saw our sign flashing in bright red lights with the names of the two R&B singers underneath. People were walking in between cars and through the busy street traffic to get in line. After minutes of stop and go traffic, I finally got into the parking lot. One of my brother's friends removed a cone from a parking spot. I parked my car in between White Boy's and B's cars. I noticed the rims add height to his car. Tone and Christian were parked next to B. Thankfully Diana didn't come because Simone was parked along with our cars.

Stepping out and locking the doors, I received some attention from some bad ass girls near the end of the line. I looked at the crowd and multiple cars entered and know our lives will soon change. I took a long look at the girls remembering their faces from Keith's club. They were wearing sexy ass outfits showing all of their goodies. Steps away from them they make it clear that they remember me also. They shout my name and taunt me showing a little skin. I took the best looking one by the hand pulling her out of line and her friends follow.

We walked past a line of people waiting and all of them stare. It felt good to be bypassing the crowd with some bad ass girls. Closer to the entrance I could hear Christian yelling over the crowd picking beautiful women and people we knew out of the line to enter. Christian squeezed by the door security rushing over to me. We hugged each other rocking back and forth.

Amad trailed behind Christian. Amad and I greeted each other but he'd quickly shifts his attention at my entourage. Amad looked at me with a surprised look and I just smiled nodding my head with approval. Amad found a way to step behind us and introduced himself to the girls.

As we walked toward the entrance I hug my brother around his neck. "Christian you have done an excellent job putting the club together. I'm proud of you."

"Reese, I have to talk to you about something later," Christian said.

"What is it man?"

"Don't worry about it right now. We'll talk later when it's just us," Christian looked behind us.

"All right bruh. Don't forget to tell me."

"You just go in here and have fun. I'll keep my eyes open."

Inside the club is how I envisioned it to be. Women from wall-to-wall, couples dancing, women dancing sexually, and dope boys popping bottles. Everyone was having a good time. Christian and Amad did a good job picking out beautiful women from the line. Women attracted money and money makes us happy.

I searched the club for the rest of the crew but the crowds made it impossible. A cocktail waitress surprises Christian and me with glasses of champagne. She pulled on Christian's jacket to get his attention. I'd over heard her telling him that she needed him to handle a problem.

"Reese, I need to talk to her. We'll talk later." Christian told me walking away with the waitress.

Suddenly some commotion from outside began to erupt. Amad told me that he'll handle the situation but whispered in my ear asking me to hook him up with one of the girls. I wave him off and turn to the girls.

"Reese, I have a bottle on ice for you at the main bar," Amad said leaving to go check on the commotion.

I'd chain-link hands with the girls and we weaved our way to the bar. Inching our way, I was being greeted by multiple people, shaking my hands, and hugging women. Two waitresses introduced themselves to me and seemed pleased to be our employees.

At the bar, the bartender stops pouring shots for a couple and rushes over to me. He places champagne glasses in front of each of the girls and pours them drinks. He introduced himself to me and grabbed two bottles of expensive champagne.

"Hey, make sure these ladies have a good time tonight. Drinks all night are free for them," I said to the bartender.

The girl whose hand I was holding becomes so excited she kisses me.

Some friends of ours, Mar and Scotty, take a seat next to me. I showed them love, hugging them both. They're high as hell and started grabbing the girls. The girls become fed up. Before leaving the best looking one asked for my number and if I could take her home tonight but I'd let her down easy. Mar told me that the crew is waiting for me in the office. I grab a bottle from the bar and looked up to see B and Tone waving for me to come up.

I tried to make my way through the crowd then Mar tapped my shoulder pointing toward the V.I.P. I couldn't see what he was pointing at so I walked toward the V.I.P with Mar and Scotty behind me. I struggled to get through the crowd but the closer I got I recognize Detective Shaw talking to a group of females whose backs were to me. Mar and Scotty headed for the office as I weaved faster through the mass of people but my view kept being intercepted. Sidestepping out of the crowd I saw Shaw leaving. Someone bumped into me causing me to lose him. Now he was nowhere in sight.

The girls remained sitting in the lounge.

Approaching the girls, they're giggling and sharing conversation. I could not hear the conversation but it was piquing my interest. I wanted to know all I can about Shaw. As I came closer, the voices became familiar. I got around to the booth and saw a pair of all too familiar crossed legs. Their laughter continued to rise until they saw me. My eyes followed up this stranger's legs meeting her eye-to-eye. I was shocked to see Simone.

Simone and Peaches sat still but Cherish choked on her drink. Peaches helped Cherish to her feet and patted her on the back. Simone got up from her seat and placed her purse on the table. Before I could ask her about Shaw, she put her lips on mine. I couldn't resist. As we'd kissed, I felt her smile. I do not know what to think of this kiss but I did want to know why she was talking to Shaw. I softly pushed her away just enough to look at her face.

"How are you and your friends doing tonight?" I asked Simone stepping away from her friends.

"We're doing fine. Amad is making sure our glasses stay full and occasionally keep us company. I haven't gone on the dance floor yet. I've been waiting for my man to come."

"Is that right? I saw you had company over here," I said.

"That was nobody."

"How do you know him?"

"I don't. He just came over here to say hi."

"You know he's a cop?"

"Yeah! He pulled me over about a month ago for speeding. I talked my way out of the ticket by giving him my number. Why are you asking me questions? When you were watching me, you should have been watching White Boy."

"Why should I watch him?" I questioned stepping closer to her.

"He's been running his mouth to Peaches about how you have been playing him with his share of the money. He's really upset at the whole crew and is plotting how to get you all," Simone replied.

"Shut that stupid shit up. He is getting paid very well. How can he complain about eating? I know your girl is making that shit up," I shake my head in disbelief.

Simone grabbed my hands. "Reese I'm just telling you this because I care about you. I don't want to see anything happen to you. If you don't believe me, then let Peaches tell you for herself."

"No don't do that. Matter of fact, don't even tell her that I know. I'm going to find out if any of this is true and if so I'll deal with it. I'll ask any of my boys if they've heard him talking shit."

Looking over Simone's shoulder, I watched Christian and Amad join her girls. Peaches whispered into Amad's ear and they'd walked away from the table. If White Boy saw this he'd act a fool. I sped through my conversation with Simone telling her about my trip tomorrow but I was distracted by the girls I came in with. Simone's jealous rage ignited. She went off asking questions about them until I clarified how I knew them. After clearing that up, she tripped about my trip with Diana. She was mad I was spending time with Diana but is even more mad I would be gone for so long. She plead with me to stay the night with her and before I had a chance to argue with her Christian interrupted us urging me to go in the office.

Amad followed us into the office and the whole crew including Mar and Scotty shouted out with excitement. Everyone greeted us with opened arms and poured champagne for us. After toasting to our new business, we shared some memories and laughs. I shared with the crew the news that I was leaving to the Bahamas tomorrow and would be gone for a week. White Boy didn't agree at first but understood when I explained from Diana's point of view. I told them I had promised her that this week will be just us and I would leave business behind meaning my phone. B helped me explain my reasons and told the crew how things will be operated while I was gone. While B was talking my phone rung. I walked away taking the call.

Diana told me she packed our luggage after Ashley went home and was now scared of being in the house alone. I checked the time. Our flight was going to leave in a few hours and I needed my rest. I told her I was leaving out right now and she became overjoyed.

"Christian, where did everybody go?" I questioned after I end the call.

"They just left. I still need to talk to you."

"Go ahead."

"Before the club became packed a waitress told me Amad and Simone were privately talking. I went to go see if it were true. I watched them for a minute then I sent the waitress back over with some drinks to do some spying. She heard them talking about some money he had paid her. To her it sounds as if it was a lot of money. Reese, you should check on that."

As I listened to Christian, my thoughts drifted. Amad was the least of my problems. My focus was on White Boy. Christian continued to rant about Amad but I ignored him overlooking the crowd watching White Boy's every move. White Boy was dancing with three girls, spilling liquor on them and on the dance floor. I signaled for Christian to take notice. I cut him off in midsentence and asked him if he had noticed anything different about White Boy. Christian said he had been doing a lot of shopping. His words caused me to become furious. He reminded me how long I had been friends with him. I gave him a hug appreciating his love for me. I told him that I would not jump to conclusions and I would talk to White Boy when I come back from my vacation. Speeding through the V.I.P lounge with Christian trying to avoid Simone and her friends. They left for the dance floor leaving their glasses and purses. I quickly noticed Simone's purse from the room. I asked for a guy selling roses to lay down a dozen roses on the table for her. I paid the man and snuck off. Before I'd left the club through the side exits a cloud of smoke blew out from a booth. We approached the booth. I was hoping it was Detective Shaw but it was Tone smoking on a blunt. I knew Tone had taken this seat to watch the exit for local robbers. Tone kept on his toes from the bullshit. He had his reasons. His uncle trusted his wife only for her to set him up with the police. Tone's uncle had been gone for five year and had eight more years remaining. Christian and Tone conversed about the club while I searched for B.

"Are you looking for your girl man?" Tone joked.

"Cut it out. I want to let B know I'm gone."

"Amad and B left about ten minutes ago. Amad said he had some bad bitches for them," Tone replied looking at his girl nervously.

"Well I'm gone. You keep an eye on that nigga man. Don't forget to buy some more work from J. That should last while I'm gone." I gave them a hug and left.

Later, before riding out to the airport I tried to call B but he didn't answer. I left a message and turn on the TV to watch my morning sports news while Diana made us breakfast. I called Keith and asked him to look over the crew while I was gone. I gave him the hotel number. He assured me he would watch over them.

Diana brought me the food but believes I was doing business so she caught an attitude aggressively shoving the plate at me. I quickly ended the call and rushed to her. Diana took my keys and waited for me in the truck. I grabbed our luggage and locked the door behind me.

CHAPTER 12

TONE

Christian and I waited outside of the club for Amad and B. Christian had finished locking the doors and was ready to leave. I told her to wait a little while longer and we would soon leave. What had me unsettled was that B left his car behind? It was unlike him to ride with some girls he didn't know. Christian told me that he had to go make the deposit before he got too tired and forgot to do it. He pulled out leaving me alone under the bright lights of the club.

"Come on Tone it's late," Lisa honk the horn begging for me to leave. I'd been waiting long enough and B will soon be here to pick up his car.

I sped to Lisa's off-campus apartment in a hurry. During the drive, Lisa gave me head causing my foot to press down on the gas getting us there in no time. We rushed taking our clothes off and diving into the bed. She straddles me, taking my dick inside her warm wet pussy. Slowly she slid up and down as I made soft moans. I tightly gripped her ass assisting her movements. Her pace gradually accelerated causing her juices to flow heavier.

Before allowing her to have an orgasm, I toss her over roughly. She looks at me with curiosity in her eyes. I open her legs spreading her pussy lips with my tongue. After eighteen long months, this is my first time going down on her. I eat her pussy forcing her to cum over and over again. She pleads for me to stop and give her some dick but I want her to remember this night.

Suddenly, my phone rings. I don't hesitate to stop causing her to let out a loud scream. I crawl over the bed to dig through my pants. I answer on the third ring.

Ashley was questioning me about B's whereabouts. I lied for him saying he has to handle some business with Amad. Ashley told me she had been calling his phone for the last four hours and he has yet to call back. She is worried that B is out fucking some other girl. I almost laughed. I made it clear B only wanted her and he was out here trying to make some money for them.

After listening to Ashley crying over the phone, I called B but I couldn't reach him either.

Lisa stretched her legs apart showing me her pussy. I leaned up against the wall grabbing myself getting hard again. She took a dildo out of her nightstand and slid the whole thing inside her. Lisa fuck the dildo as if it was me.

I left a message for B then hurried back jumping in the bed with her.

In the middle of the afternoon the next day, Lisa and I rush to get dressed. Her class starts in an hour and we're thirty minutes away from the campus.

Before I dropped her off, I sped into the club parking lot and came to a screeching halt barely missing B's car. I hopped out and checked to make sure I didn't scratch his car. The smoke from the breaks choked me up. I left a skid mark on the pavement. I circled the truck opening the passenger door. Lisa looked at me crazy but I didn't respond. I pulled out my gun from the glove compartment and walked back to B's car checking for any signs of anyone trying to break in. After looking inside the windows and checking the door locks I knew no one has touched the car.

Crash!!! The sound of glass breaking cames from the back of the club.

I'd rapidly race toward the back of the building with my aim held steady. I couldn't believe a burglar decided to break in during the middle of the afternoon. I walked by the side entrance. The doors locked.

Searching for any sign of the sound, I couldn't find any broken glass nor broken windows.

CRASH! Again the sound of broken glass…

Reaching the back parking lot I saw broken glass shattered all over the pavement. I slowly walked over to the dumpster and a bum pops out. We scared each other half to death.

"Oh shit!" I shouted.

I grabbed him by his filthy hood. I place the barrel of the gun directly to his head.

"I'm sorry. I'm sorry," The man cried.

"What in the fuck are you doing back here?" I stare him down.

"I just wanted to collect some cans so I can buy me something to eat."

I eased away the gun from his head," I own this club and I thought someone was breaking in my shit. I apologize if I scared you but I'm not letting anyone get in my shit."

"It's okay. I've had many guns pulled on me in my day. So you own this club too?" he climbed out.

"Too…?"

"Yeah, a short muscular man told me last night to get off the premises."

"Oh yeah…, that must have been B."

"He told me to leave because I was asking the lovely ladies for money."

"Do me a favor, you clean this shit up and come back, I'll have a job for you. Ask for Christian. He'll give you everything you need to keep my lot clean. Here's a hundred dollars for you. Get you a hot meal and some clean clothes. I'm looking forward to seeing you sir."

"Oh thank you!" he cheerfully shouted.

My horn blared. I turned away from him and rush toward the truck.

"Wait, I almost forgot to ask," the bum added.

"What up?"

"Is your friend okay? I saw him arguing with a group of guys. Then he climbed in the back of their truck."

Who were these muthafuckas B had beef with? Lisa honk the horn rapidly. I'd ran back toward the truck.

"God bless you!" the man shouted from a distance.

I drove her to campus. She asked if I could bring Mar over later in the week to chill with her and her room-mate. I said yes but she knew my answer could change at any time.

As I was pulling away, Ashley called me and said she had received a call from some nigga claiming that he had B. She thought it was one of us fucking with her until the caller demanded for some ransom money or they would kill B. I tried to calm her down and assure her we would get him back soon. I could barely understand her words because she would not quit crying. I told her I was on my way but I had to inform the crew, so we could handle things swiftly. I ended the call and sped through the streets toward the spot.

I walked in with anger. White Boy and Amad was playing a videogame while smoking weed. I stepped in front of the TV getting their immediate attention. They asked me to move but I stood my ground staring down Amad.

"Where is B?" I asked.

"Why are you asking me nigga?"

"Nigga because you were the last one with him last night…!" I shout balling my fist.

"Man I don't know what to tell you. I introduced him to a girl from the club and I went my way and he went his. We were supposed to meet up at the same hotel but I guess he went home."

"The nigga didn't go home! His girl has been calling me all night worried about his ass."

"Well shit he is probably still fucking that bitch. Now watch out so I can finish beating this nigga's ass."

I leapt over the table swinging at Amad. White boy hopped up off the couch and backs away. Amad and I trade punches. I pounded my fist against his body causing him to try to guard without trading back punches. I'd let up and yell at him again asking about B.

"Nigga I know that you know what happened to B!" I aggressively bark at Amad.

Amad reached inside the couch and pulls out his gun. I'm stunned by his actions. I don't hear what he is saying but I like what I see. I commend his passion for his defense and tell them what Ashley had said. I tell them I want to be over Ashley's house for the next time that the kidnappers call.

We went over to Ashley and B's house and sat with her waiting for the next call. She was mourning like he was already dead. Ashley told White Boy about the phone call she had received. She told us that the caller knew us very well.

"Ashley, we'll get B back. Don't worry about it. He'll be home," I said trying to calm her down.

White Boy poured her a glass of wine. Ashley sat on the couch crying her eyes out trying to calm down by drinking the glass. Her phone suddenly rung. After she took a look at the number, she passes me the phone. I answered the phone and recognize the caller is no other than Big Mike.

Big Mike told me he wanted $500,000 for B. I asked him was this about the bricks we took from him and he just laughed in my ear. White Boy overheard who I was talking to and became furious. Mike heard White Boy in the background talking shit and he told me that he couldn't wait to bury him. I didn't want to hear another word from him but I also didn't want to anger him knowing that my boy's life was in his hands. I'd play it cool telling him we'll have the money.

CHAPTER 13

TONE

White Boy and I come back home and flood the streets with work. We went back to our old means of hustling, cooking up cocaine to get all of that extra money we don't usually make. I was a chef in the kitchen almost doubling the amount of crack cocaine out of soft cocaine. The heroin will hopefully speed up the process to get the ransom money.

We sold to our crews and we beg them to buy more at a cheaper price. Mar and White Boy have been going from spot to spot selling as much as they can. Together they're getting rid of the dope, but it's not coming fast enough.

I sit alone in the office contemplating how we'll get the rest of this money before the due date.

Amad barges through the office door laughing and drinking out of a bottle of expensive champagne. I look at him as if he is crazy. He asked me why I was looking so depressed. He tries to cheer me up telling me that the club is full and we're making a lot of money tonight.

To me the money that we're making tonight is pennies compared to what we need yet, a couple hundred thousand.

"Do I need to remind you of how much we need to pay Big Mike? I asked Amad staring him in the eyes.

He smiled.

"My boys want to spend $200,000 with us."

I jumped up from my chair and hug Amad with joy.

After we close the club, Amad and I waited for his boys at a popular restaurant parking lot next to the 75/70 interstate. Amad asked to listen to my music but I rejected his requests telling him I wanted us to stay focused. I stayed on my guard, checking my mirrors and surroundings periodically.

Amad's boys called him saying they're here. I watched them pulled directly in front of the restaurant next to the handicapped lots. Amad ended the call and told me his boys only wanted him to do the transaction. I told him the only way that we would do business with them was only for me to go. He called them back and told them that I was bringing the dope or we wasn't doing business. Amad signaled for me to go motioning with his hands to get up and go.

I walked toward their SUV and Amad turned up the volume in my car causing customers to stop and stare. I climbed in the backseat and shook their hands before setting the dope next to me. The passenger told me the money for the dope was under the driver seat. Smiling, I bent over. After grabbing the duffel bag, I sat up to see the passenger had his pistol dead in my face. I'd slowly put my hands in the air staring him in the eye. He ordered for me to give him the dope.

The next time I saw these niggas they will be dead. I reminded them that they were in my city and I would soon find them.

They ignored my threats and forced me out. The passenger rolled down his window maintaining aim on me through the parking lot. I searched the parking lot and saw a family parking a few feet behind me so I couldn't pull out and shoot them. I stood still until I was out of his range and then rushed to the truck.

I slammed the door. Amad asked me multiple questions but I was too busy trying to catch up with them. I was stuck at a traffic light behind other drivers. Impatiently I got out of line and drove into oncoming traffic. I managed to weave out of traffic and back on the right side of the street. Reaching the exit not knowing which way they went. We rode up 75 for about twenty minutes not able to find them. Feeling an empty feeling inside my stomach knowing they got away. I thought of all the exits that they could have taken and maybe they hopped on 70.

Amad finally turned down the music and told me to give up.

"Tone they're gone fam…," Amad said basically telling me what I was thinking. He tries calling them repeatedly but of course they didn't answer.

The next exit I pulled off the highway. At the light I punched the dashboard so hard Amad jumped out his seat. I stared out the windshield with cold eyes trying to get my thoughts straight. Amad passed his blunt to me. As I inhaled and exhaled the smoke my mind races. How am I going to get the ransom money?

Back on the highway heading into the city, Amad and I didn't speak. I was upset with him although what happened isn't his fault. I was mainly upset at myself for being so damn greedy.

Amad's phone rung. I'd mute the music so I could be able to hear his conversation but unfortunately the call wasn't his boys, its White Boy. White Boy was telling Amad about his bad luck trying to make some money at a dice game in the hood. He felt lucky after winning at the casino and thought he could help raise some money by gambling.

Some heavy gamblers played where he was shooting dice at. These niggas like to show off their money by taking others. I had plans to take theirs.

White Boy asked Amad for money to try to get back what he lost or he would have to put up his car. I could hear in his voice that he was furious.

I got on the phone with him and told him I had a plan. White Boy was with it of course.

Amad and I went by Mar's spot to get some heavy artillery.

Mar hands me an AR15 and wondered what was up. I assured him that we would handle it and if we needed any help I would call. He wanted to go with us badly but I decided against it not wanting any bloodshed.

I sent White Boy a text message telling him we were coming. We planned to have the door entrance cleared and unlocked for an easy entrance, parking around the corner from White Boy. I covered my face for protection and put my gloves on. Amad had his gun out ready and loaded. I took the machine gun from the backseat and swiftly exit the truck. Amad and I rapidly run through neighboring yards until we reached the porch of the house.

Cautiously, I look inside the window watching two dice games being played with niggas side betting. I counted about twelve people inside. I signal Amad. Without hesitation, he darts inside grabbing the first person he saw.

I ordered the men to place everything on the tables while trying to keep aim on each of them. I look over at White Boy. His eyes grow wider the more I shout my demands. I turned to peek behind me for Amad. Out of the darkness a young skinny muthafucka had his gun aimed on me. Amad slapped him behind the head knocking him to the floor.

The men faces had now changed from happiness to fright seeing that we were not playing. They take off their jewelry and place their money on the pool tables. Amad walked behind each of them patting them down making sure everything was out. I found a large trash bag in the kitchen. When I reentered the room Amad was trying to make White Boy give up his chain. I had to resist myself from laughing as White Boy reluctantly gave up his necklace. We rushed out the house as fast as we came in.

We met back at the spot to count the money. Amad had already decided on what jewelry he wanted to keep. I reminded him that we needed every dollar for the ransom but he felt as if he should get something comparing himself to White Boy. He told me he deserved something for his hard work. I agreed not wanting to argue any further.

White Boy entered the house wanting to know how much we made believing that it was six figures plus. I told him that we only took $60,000 and maybe another $40,000 in jewelry.

He looked at me with disbelief.

"That's it?"

"That's it," I said with a resentful look tossing the last stack on the table.

White Boy picked up two stacks of cash and slapped them against the palm of his hand.

"Y'all niggas are tripping! We just hit them niggas for $60,000 and y'all are mad," Amad interjected.

"Nigga this ain't shit! We have two days to get this money. Them bitch ass niggas should've had more money than that!" White Boy shouts. He throws the money across the room. "Fuck! I have a way for us to get the money," He bobbed his head.

"How…?" I asked.

"I know some Hispanic muthafuckas who are really getting it. We can take their dope and their money. You see how easy it is. Let's do it."

CHAPTER 14

TONE

It was Saturday night and I decided to keep the club open. White Boy had a plan for us to have all of the money by tonight. White Boy, Amad, and Mar waited for me in the parking lot. I finish giving Christian direction about the club and walk out to the boys.

White Boy reminded us of why we were robbing muthafuckas tonight. "I have been watching three spots that we can hit and get some quick money."

I could feel his passion to get our boy back. He knew we were going to go along with his plan because this was what White Boy and Mar did best. Robbing…

The first two spots we hit were easy. Both of them are stash houses hiding bags of cash and work with minimum security. I estimated that we had made about the $200,000 we had lost. I want more. I wanted somebody to feel my pain and suffer the depression I went through.

"This one won't be any walk in the park," White Boy says. "These niggas will be ready and heavily secured."

At the final spot I parked behind White Boy so we could have a good view on the house.

Time was quickly passing by. It was two o'clock in the morning and their spot still had constant traffic. The traffic wasn't dope fiends but niggas who are out here getting money like us.

Watching people go in and out exchanging bags of money for drugs was weighing on my patience. My adrenaline was pumping so fast through my veins I couldn't sit still.

Mar reached down to get his AR. We covered our faces with a mask and checked our weapons. One last guy walked out speeding off in his car. I sped in front of the house. White Boy and Amad pulled up right behind me.

Leaving our rides running in the middle of the dark streets, we hopped out. I gave the door two hard kicks knocking it down. Three Hispanic men scattered through the house but they were not able to get far before White Boy and Mar caught up with them. They stared them down with the barrel of their guns.

Amad and I chased the third guy through the house but he is able to make it to a bedroom. We threaten him to come out or he'll be shot. He threatened us back which just added fuel to the fire for me.

"God please watch over me. I need you now." I silently prayed before shooting toward the voice. I stood above him about to empty out the clip but Amad urged for me to leave. I glanced over my shoulder to see Amad with a duffel bag over his shoulder.

Mar stood next to him with a bag in his hand.

"Tone come on. We got the shit now let's go!" Mar shouted.

Looking down at the man struggling to breath, I decided to spare his life. I felt at ease watching someone else experience pain.

When we got back to the spot, I sat in silence with the thought of Ashley stressing out and worse my boy being tortured by Big Mike's men. I raised my head from staring at the floor and noticed White Boy standing before me.

"Tone we're going to get B back man. I already know what you are thinking," White Boy speaks sympathetically.

"Man I'm going to kill every last one of them niggas," I replied.

Mar walked over to us.

"Are you good bruh? Don't let these niggas win man. We'll get them muthafuckas."

"I'll be all right when we get our boy back. This whole situation is just getting to me. I can't wait to see Big Mike's fat ass dying."

"How about we all get out of here and go to Keith's so we can clear our minds," Mar suggested.

"Yeah, we can do that. I'll drive."

White Boy called Keith in advance to let him know that we were on our way. Keith was happy to hear from us and wanted to talk to us anyway. We all climbed in my truck and headed to Keith's.

****

Jasmine met us at the entrance and escorts us to our V.I.P room. We were greeted with a stripper for each of us but two of them walked over to White Boy like he was a celebrity. Jasmine just laughed as she left the room but promises to send another girl to accommodate us.

We all were having a good time drinking and fooling around with the women but I couldn't get my head on straight. I took a seat close to the stage in order to get myself together. Mar followed behind me. We were surrounded by horny men shouting at the women. I continued to sip on my beer enjoying the performance of two strippers' ass clapping together competing for Mar's money. He tossed a few bills onto the stage and came back to accompany me.

Mar asked, "What is up with Tasha?"

Tasha was Lisa's roommate. I remembered telling him they wanted us to come over tonight after we were done handling business. Mar and Tasha met one day he had rode with me to their apartment to give Lisa some money. Mar got her number and after that they hooked up from time to time. Tasha only wanted dick and money but Mar didn't give a fuck.

127

This nigga would come to the spot with videos of her having sex with him and other bitches. The nigga is wild.

I called Lisa.

"Hey baby what's up?" Lisa asked with laughter.

"Nothing much, just handling business with the crew. Shit, Mar and I was hoping to come through and kick it with you and Tasha."

"Well…" she said unsure.

"Well what?" I spat.

"She has some company over now but baby I still want to see you."

"I'm supposed to come over there by myself when there is some other niggas there. You know I cannot walk into darkness like that."

"I want to see you." Lisa plead in a soft voice.

"Let us finish up here and I will give you a call when I'm on my way," I end the call.

Keith walked over and embraces us. "Let's talk in my office. It's more private."

We'd follow him and take our seats. Keith told us all that he knew about our business. He questioned my sanity with hearing about all of the shit I was doing. He understood the pressure I was under with holding the team down while Reese was gone. To my surprise Ashley had called Keith numerous of times hoping that he could help her. I sat with a blank look listening to Keith trying to motivate me to get back on track. He stopped talking and pulls out his phone.

Mar and I looked at each other not knowing who he was calling. Keith could call a gang of goons right now to handle us or our problem.

He pushed away from the desk to lean back in his chair. Keith changed the sound of his voice into a proper business man. He requested to be connected to room 568 and asked for Reese or Diana. Keith never ceased to amaze me, having ways to get in contact with anybody.

Keith and Reese's conversation didn't last long. He told Reese the main points of how things are going on with the crew without saying much over the phone. Coming from Keith, nothing else needs to be said.

Soon as he ended his call with Reese, I received a call from a strange number.

"Hello," I spoke with caution.

"Tone it's me," Reese said.

Reese said Keith had put him on game about everything and would be flying out in the morning. He wanted everyone to be at the spot early tomorrow afternoon. Reese said he had a plan that he wanted everyone to listen to. Before he ended our call he reminded me to calm down knowing how I could get.

After thanking Keith, Mar and I walked out of the office to get White Boy and Amad. They were having a ball with the ladies. White Boy tried to persuade me to stay, telling me that I could enjoy myself with them and the strippers. He joked about me wanting to go over Lisa's, saying these bitches can do more here than she could.

All of my boys had only seen Lisa's quiet side. They did not know how she was a freak in the bed. He got Mar to join him with the joke. I figured the alcohol was talking for them. I walked over to White Boy throwing my arm over his shoulder escorting him to the truck.

I blasted my music speeding out of the parking lot. My phone rung. I answered the phone thinking it was Lisa but to my surprise it was Ashley. Ashley said that Mike has called her once again to remind her of the deadline. I told her that we have the money and everything will be okay. Ashley thanked me for being such a good friend.

Since we were only blocks from Lisa's apartment, I decided against calling her so I could surprise her with my presence.

Slowly driving through Lisa's parking lot I tried to find a spot to park. I crept pass by an SUV that gives me a sense of alert. I slammed on the brakes.

"Tone what the fuck man! I almost spilled my weed." White Boy said with a frown.

"Did y'all see the truck back there?" I questioned with excitement.

Mar sat up in his seat, turning around to look. "Which one…?" I was speeding rapidly in reverse braking at the tail of the SUV. Everyone again shouted at me with frustration. I pointed at the truck. White Boy turned his head to look over and dropped his blunt on the floor pouring out all the weed. Amad's face held an expression of disbelief. Mar knew what time it was and prepared himself.

I thought of different ways to kill these niggas. A knot developed in my stomach knowing it was time to go to work. The SUV was parked next to Tasha's piece of shit car. Right then I knew these niggas were in Lisa's apartment. I dialed Lisa's number.

As I waited for Lisa to answer, White Boy was getting hyped up to get them. He was telling Amad and Mar how he had not ever trusted Amad's boys since the first meeting. Mar was feeding off of White Boy's energy. Amad sat with his face covered. White Boy slightly opened the door but I stopped him telling him that I wanted to make sure that things are done right.

"We don't need any witnesses or need to make any mistakes when we take these niggas out," I said looking at them.

Lisa answered on the last ring before her phone went to voicemail.

"Hi baby are you on your way yet? These lames are over here talking shit about what they got and putting down the city like niggas don't get it here."

"Oh yeah…," Her words added to my anger.

"Yes, Tasha is biting because these dudes are from out of town."

"Your friend ain't shit. All she want from a nigga is dick and money. That is the only reason why she is on Mar so hard but he knows what time it is."

"Yeah my girl is a big hoe." Lisa chuckled.

"Do she have a nigga for you over there?" I asked trying to get some info.

"If that's what you want to call it. I want to see you."

"All right we're leaving from the club now. Give me about ten minutes to get there."

"Who is we Tone?"

"Lisa, I'm on my way. You say you want to see me so I'm leaving right now and I'm bringing my boys," I snapped back at her.

"Is White Boy with you? Tone please don't let him come over here on his bullshit," Lisa pleaded.

"That's my nigga and yes he is coming. If you are so worried about him you should ask your company to leave."

"I guess I don't have any choice because I know how he is," she ends the call.

We waited patiently for the first sight of them. I had the music damn near on mute. Mar and White Boy were discussing tactics amongst themselves but I did not allow their conversation to break my concentration.

Minutes later the building door swung open. I was sitting on the edge of my seat gripping the handle of the gun.

"Tone is that them?" Mar asked.

I didn't answer watching the nigga who put his gun in my face. I wanted to walk up and blow his brains out over the concrete. He is all over Tasha as they walk toward the SUV. The multiple chains around his neck make him a more intriguing target.

"What are we waiting for?" White Boy stepped out.

"Hold up!" Mar said.

Tasha embraces the guy and gives him a passionate kiss.

"Look at this gold digging bitch," Mar laughs.

When they separate, Tasha jogs back into the apartment. The two of them get into their SUV and quickly pull off.

White Boy climbed back inside the truck and I pressed down on the gas to catch up with them. In no time we were right behind them like a lion sneaking up on their prey. White Boy wanted me to pull up on the side of them so he could empty his clip inside the car but I told him to wait for the perfect opportunity.

Twenty minutes of following them while maintaining our stealth I become impatient. White Boy continued to rant on how we should get them but I shut him out trying to think. Mar broke my thoughts pointing out how they were swerving over the streets. The driver probably had one too many drinks kicking it with Tasha. I looked around for the police hoping they were not around to pull him over.

White Boy sat up in his seat. He became cheerful thinking that we'd be able to hit them easily.

"Come on Tone catch them muthafuckas!" White Boy urged me jumping in his seat.

I sped up not because of White Boy, but to make sure we didn't get caught by the light since they'll probably speed through the caution light. The driver slammed down on his brakes through. Pulling right behind them so my lights blind them. I saw the driver trying to shield his eyes in the rearview mirror.

White Boy taps on Mar's shoulder, "Get ready, we're about to handle these niggas."

"These muthafuckas have now slipped!" White Boy said sternly climbing out.

"What are you about to do?" Amad asked.

White Boy crept alongside the truck.

"Tone are you going to let him do this in the middle of the street?" Amad looked at me nervously.

I get my gun from the glove compartment and set myself to shoot out the window. Mar sneaked out leaving his door slightly open. He and White Boy sprinted on opposite side of their SUV. The sound of boots smacking against the pavement was all to be heard in the night air.

I looked up. In a matter of seconds our light will change. When the light turned green, White Boy and Mar have their guns looking down on them.

White Boy opened the driver's door and pulled him out of the SUV while keeping aim on his head. I stepped out to assist White Boy but he was already escorting the driver back to me. I forced my gun against the driver's neck and threw him in the back with Amad. White Boy took the driver seat of their SUV. Mar snatched the passenger in the back seat with him so he could be able to keep a close eye on him.

133

I watched the driver in my rearview mirror. He remained still and quiet. I looked ahead and see Mar is landing punches on his partner. My phone rings. It's White Boy.

"What up?" I asked.

"Tone, this bitch ass nigga is going to lead us to their spot. We're going to get all of our shit back plus whatever they have."

"All right keep your eyes on him. He is a snake."

"Don't worry about him. Mar has him under control. You should see Mar rocking his head right now," White Boy chuckled.

"Y'all don't kill the nigga."

We drove and finally arrive in front of a brick townhouse. The house was dark and I warned White Boy to be careful just in case this is a trap. White Boy and Mar closely walked behind the passenger and they enter the house. Mar stepped back out waving for me to come inside. Amad and I got out but I had a sudden thought to tell Amad to wait out here. I wanted Amad to be our look out while we handled these muthafuckas. I reminded myself of the last time I had let him be alone; I ordered for Amad to stay focused and not to play any music.

"If we're not out within five minutes come in blasting," I instructed Amad giving him a dead stare so that he knows I'm serious.

The driver kept stumbling over his feet, so it takes us more time than I expected to get inside the house. When we finally get inside I shove him down on the couch next to his boy. He tries to stand back up but Mar hits him with a powerful right hook to the jaw, sitting his ass back down. White Boy rushes down the stairs. I ask him if he has found our money yet and he says no. I tell them that the money is in the house somewhere we just need to find it quickly.

"This nigga acting like he don't talk," Mar pointed at the nigga who robbed me.

The passenger sat up with a screwed up face bravely staring me down.

White Boy stood next to me, "Oh you don't want to talk. I have ways to make muthafuckas talk."

"No, I got him."

Without hesitation, I pulled my gun out shooting him above his knee.

He yelled out in agony tumbling down to the floor. White Boy kicked him hard as hell in the ribs to add to his pain. He continued to yell in agony so I placed the barrel into his mouth.

"Now do you want to talk muthafuckas!" I bend over staring him in his eyes.

"Kill this bitch ass nigga Tone!" White Boy barked.

"No, no, no don't kill my brother," the driver begs. "I'll give you your shit back plus some money if you just let him live. We'll even disappear tomorrow."

"Someone take his ass to get our shit," I said.

Mar and White Boy takes the drunken driver to a room in the back. I nod to assure him that I won't harm his brother.

Soon as I pulled the gun away from his face he built up enough courage to speak.

"Yo son, you know you are fucking with the wrong man's money."

"You think that I give a fuck? You are lucky that you are still breathing."

"You'll give a fuck when Big Mike kills your ass!" He spat.

Confusion scattered my mind wondering how these niggas knew Big Mike. Maybe everything was set up for them to rob us for him. Big Mike didn't want B or the money he wanted to see us suffer. Amad introduced us to these niggas. The fact that Amad was the last one to be with B stuck out in my head. If I found out he had anything to do with either situation he would be a dead man.

Amad crept inside with his eyes wide opened staring at me standing over his so-called friend. I was about to pull the trigger but decided not to. Because the way I saw it, if Amad's not guilty, he should take care of them. It was his people, his fault.

"Take him to the back with his brother. I want you to kill both of them," I instructed.

"Why? Let's get the shit and leave."

"Did you know that these niggas work for Big Mike?"

Amad doesn't say a word looking at me with confusion.

"Nigga did you hear me?"

"No Tone, I didn't know."

White Boy walks into the room with what seems to be my duffel bag. "What's going on?"

"These muthafuckas work for Mike!" I yell.

"Tone you know that just made this meeting a lot better. I'll handle them," White Boy says.

"No. Amad will do it. I want you to make sure he get the job done."

Amad and White Boy dragged the nigga across the floor into the bedroom. He is squirming trying to get away I follow behind them and notice the room has been trashed. White Boy instructed Amad on how to kill these niggas. I leave and open the door to the truck. I hear two shots fired. Boom! Boom! I climbd in the truck filling a sense of satisfaction.

CHAPTER 15

REESE

Diana and I finally arrived back home after our early morning flight. She is mad as hell about us having to cut our vacation short. Diana wanted for us to spend each day relaxing and enjoying each other's company. She heard my conversation with Keith and Tone so she knew it was urgent for me to come home. We didn't talk much on the flight home or during the drive. I knew my business was taking a toll on our relationship and soon I would have to decide on what is important in my life but today wasn't the day.

Besides the circumstances, it felt good to be home. I felt a sense of comfort walking into my home. Watching Diana move around the house was making me horny. We had sex every day but our positions were limited due to her pregnancy. We were still able to make good love. Now that we were home I wanted her to do some freaky shit. Knowing she would feel uncomfortable doing something out of the ordinary, I'd let go of the idea. Simone crossed my mind and I began to think about her sexy body and the way she worked it when we were fucking.

"Reese, I'm tired from the flight. I'm going upstairs to take a nap before my sister picks me up for the afternoon service." Diana interrupted my thoughts.

"Okay. I'll be up to unpack."

Diana slowly walked up the stairs. "You should come with us. It will be good for you." she suggested.

"C'mon, you know I can't go. I have too much shit to do. B is waiting for me to get him before some nigga kill him. Besides, God gave up on me a long time ago." I replied sadly but meaning every word.

Diana stops halfway up the steps. "You sound stupid Reese. God will never give up on you. It is you who has given up on Him. Before you leave out the door, you should talk to him. In fact, I'll talk to him for you."

"I'll be okay."

"I know you are tight with B but why do you have to be the one who handles everything? You should let somebody else get him back," she cried.

"I can't. I have to do this shit. He would not have gotten kidnapped if I didn't go on that stupid trip."

My words hurt her feelings. She stormed up the stairs and slammed the door behind her.

I sat on the couch, feeling bad for hurting her. I searched through my phone for floral companies so I could send her some flowers to make up. My voicemail icon popped up. Listening to the messages, I heard a message from Simone, two from the crew, and one from Big Mike. Mike tried to tell me that he had control over the situation and demanded his ransom money. I laughed. He wanted to get my attention and pay me back. Well I was going to give him my attention.

I became so stressed between the argument, listening to the crews messages and now Big Mike I needed a stress reliever. I picked the phone back up and call Simone.

"It is about time you decided to call me," Simone said with an attitude.

"I just got back. Did you miss me?" I asked playfully.

"No, I didn't miss you. I missed that dick," she laughed.

"Oh, is that right? How about I come over later tonight after I take care of some business?"

"Umm, how about we get a room?" Simone asked in a sexy voice.

"Yeah we can do that but you know I can't stay."

"Why? Your girl don't want to share you." Simone laughed harder now.

"Stop talking about her." I snapped.

"Damn, why are you getting so defensive? I was thinking she could join us, if that's something you would want. I know how to share."

I thought about the idea of having them together. "She isn't for anything like that."

"That's too bad. I wanted to formally introduce myself to her. She could have tasted me for herself and found out why you can't get enough," Simone joked.

Before I could respond, Diana was standing behind me on the stairs. "Reese, who are you talking to?" she said walking toward me.

I hesitated to speak to her so I told Simone that I would talk to her later.

"No, you don't have to call her back. I know that it's that girl." Diana attempted to reach for the phone but I leaned back out of her reach.

"Reese if you don't give me that damn phone!" She climbed on my lap, snatched the phone out of my hands, and then walked away.

Diana sat at the dining room table secretively talking to Simone.

What could Simone be telling her? I didn't want to seem nervous so I waited for her to get off the phone.

Five minutes later, she walked back over nicely and handed the phone over. She didn't say a word to me as she went back upstairs. I followed her to the bedroom and went straight into our walk-in closet to change my clothes. I put on an all-black outfit and arm myself. Diana looked at me nervously as I loaded each bullet. I called Tone and told him the plan for tonight. Then I called Big Mike.

He answered on the first ring.

"You finally received my message," he chuckled.

"Yeah, I got it!"

"What's up with all of the hostility? You should be relaxed from your vacation with your woman."

"Mike leave my girl out of this shit. All we need to talk about is when and where we need to meet!" I said sternly.

"Listen to you now Reese. You are the man now. New connect. New workers. You have all you need in this world. Nice house, beautiful girl and you are about to be a family man. Did you think I'll let your punk ass niggas rob me and I wouldn't do anything about it? I have a reputation Reese."

"Mike we have your money. I want to get my nigga back."

"That's what I always liked about you Reese. You have a good heart and you're always about business. Let's meet at the usual spot in two hours. By the way, don't forget to bring that bitch White Boy with you!" Big Mike spat then ends the call.

Getting ready to leave, I passed by the bathroom and notice Diana curling her hair. I stand next to her to get her attention and she gives me a kiss goodbye.

As I drove to meet the crew over at the location, I received a call from Simone. She told me she reserved a room for tonight because White Boy and Peaches would be there doing their thing. She told me what Peaches has planned for White Boy. That Peaches was a super freak even more than her. Peaches was going to show White Boy that side of her tonight. I told Simone I would see her.

141

Pulling in front of the spot, I notice how the sun was beginning to set. The clock was ticking on B's life and we had to act soon. Becoming heated when I saw my brother's car in the driveway. I had tried over and over again to keep my lifestyle from him but he insisted on being around the game.

I walked in the house with an attitude but seeing the crew together to handle Big Mike changed my feelings immediately. I showed love to everyone but, Amad's wasn't here. I wondered where he could've been at a time when we needed him most but I didn't become discourage.

"Amad called me earlier saying things are to out-of-control for him and he is done," White Boy announced.

"What the fuck is he talking about?" I'd looked around the room.

"We had to handle his people last night. While you were gone, they robbed me and we had to put in work to get the money back for Braylon," Tone said.

"Did y'all handle them niggas?"

"Yeah we got them," Mar replied.

"I made Amad take care of them," Tone add.

"Reese you know Amad isn't built for this shit. He is probably somewhere hiding like a little bitch," Mar interjected.

White Boy blew out a stream of smoke, "Yeah, he told me he isn't going to kill anybody else and some bullshit about having to watch his back."

"What?" I questioned.

"Man that muthafucka is scared. Last night shook his ass up. He said he's going to stay out of the way at least until this shit is over," White Boy tapped his ashes into an ashtray.

"That shit doesn't sound right to me. He has been acting strange on some secretive shit." I stood up.

"Reese I also found out the niggas he introduced us to were also fucking with Big Mike," Tone looked me in the eye.

I looked over at Scotty. "Scotty, I know you have something on your mind to tell me. You always keep your eyes open on everything."

"It does not sound right to me either, too coincidental. If you want me to Reese, I can cancel this problem for you," Scotty stated simply.

I take a deep breath and then exhale, "We will deal with Amad after we get B back. If Amad has anything to do with B, I was sure that B would like to get Amad himself."

"So Reese, tell us how you want to kill Big Mike's fat ass?" White Boy asked.

I told the crew my plan and Christian wonders what he could do for us. I asked him to go home and to open the club tomorrow. Christian believed he was a man and could handle his own. He wanted to help the team as much as he could. This was the life he wanted to live. I told Christian to stay at the spot and if Amad happened to come, he was ordered to keep him there. Christian accepted this responsibility and now was in the game.

CHAPTER 16

REESE

Two hours after talking to Mike, we met him and his men at the warehouse. Big Mike's Hummer sat in between two Range Rovers. Their headlights are beaming on us as we'd parked. Tone pulled up alongside of me and waited for my direction. Big Mike's men climbed out of their trucks and posted positions. He brought extra protection. He hadn't had this much protection since our first time doing business years ago.

White Boy and I stepped out of my truck and the others followed. Soon as our feet hit the pavement Big Mike's men had their weapons aimed on us. I looked over at White Boy and his face showed nothing but anger. White Boy told me that the nigga by Mike's Hummer was at the meeting when they first put Amad's boys on. White Boy whispered to me that he wished he would have killed him then. I'd shook my head knowing what he was capable of. White Boy and the nigga stared each other down. Tone took notice and his face quickly turned into a frown. He obviously remembered him too.

"White Boy you'll get your chance to get him along with the rest of these muthafuckas. We're going to stick to the plan but I want you to take his muthafucking wig off!" I said sternly.

Big Mike climbed out. He talked to the guard whom White Boy was watching, then looked over at us laughing. White Boy's finger inched closer to the trigger, I signaled for him to remain patient.

"Reese, I see you have some new members to your crew. Oh and you brought my favorite bitch with you. White Boy, how have you been?" Big Mike laughed harder.

White Boy's red face screwed up more.

"Mike let's do this shit so we can both get back to business." I walked toward him with the bags of money.

Big Mike continued to laugh but settled down when I stopped in front of him. He shook my hand and embraced me like he was genuinely happy to see me.

"Reese, climb in so we can talk business."

Big Mike entered behind me leaving enough room for me to place the bags in-between us. The nigga who White Boy was staring down shut the door behind us. When the door closes, I unzipped the bags. Big Mike randomly pulled out stacks and flipped through them checking the bills. My hands sweat as anxiety built inside me.

"Reese, I'd always loved how you conducted your business son. I didn't want things to come down to this. We were making money for each other. I couldn't hold my head high as a man if I allowed somebody to rob me and get away with it. I could have had your whole team killed a long time ago but I wanted to enjoy getting you muthafuckas back."

"Where is B?"

"He is safe."

"I came to give you your money so that I can get my nigga back."

"You can keep the money if you do me a favor." Big Mike said with a suspicious look on his face.

"What are you talking about?" I inquired.

"Take care of White Boy for me and I'll make sure your family will be taken care of."

"No, I'll make sure of that!" I said aggressively.

"Like how you look after B?" Big Mike chuckled.

"I made my decision."

"A'ight, since I'm a man of my word, I'll give you B back." He takes out his phone and demands for the kidnappers to release B.

"Mike let me talk to B so I can make sure he is okay," I interrupted his conversation.

"Put that nigga on the phone real quick," Mike handed me the phone.

I heard someone on the other end fumble the phone. "B!"

"What up Reese? When are you coming to get my muthafucking ass?" B mumbled. He sounded fatigued.

"Soon man, don't worry about shit."

"I'm hungrier than a muthafucka. These bitch made muthafuckas don't feed a nigga much. They tried to fuck me up but you know I can take a punch. I'll be alright soon as I see my bitch. How is she? I bet she is going crazy."

"You know how she is but she'll be happy to see you. I have some things to finish up but I need you to call me when you are safe before I pass over all of this money."

"Handle your business. As you know by now, I have some business to handle with Amad soon as I get home."

"Right, let me do this shit and I'll holla at you soon."

Big Mike took the phone back and instructed his men to release B. I sat listening to what would be his last words. He ended his call and confessed to me how much he thought he knew us. I'd think to myself that he didn't know us well enough because in a matter of seconds he would be dead. He continued to talk reckless about White Boy. His grudge with him was off of the charts. Mike again asked me to change my mind and trade the money for White Boy but I gently let him down.

My phone interrupted our conversation. B said the kidnappers dropped him off at a rest stop between Springfield and Columbus. I told him he would be picked up within thirty minutes.

Big Mike finished running his mouth and tried to convince me to change my mind. He took his eyes off me for a second and I pulled out my gun and shot his driver once in the back of his head. The driver's brains splattered over the windshield as his body fell against the steering wheel causing the horn to scream. Gunshots echoed the parking lot. I turned toward Big Mike and his eyes are shocked with surprise. I forcefully put the gun to his neck and took the bags from his grasp. Mike begged for his life which fell on deaf ears.

Moments later the parking lot became silent and so did his words. The only sound left was the horn. White Boy pulled open the door and a cold breeze enters the truck. Mar stood behind White Boy with a gasoline container.

"Oh, if it ain't my bitch," Big Mike said sarcastically.

"Yeah the same bitch that is about to fuck you." White Boy replied.

"Do what you have to do because my bitch will get you and Reese," Big Mike fixed his suit.

Laughing at Mike's comment, I exit the Hummer but I did wonder if he had someone else watching us. I walked toward the truck, stop, turn around and watched Mar pour gasoline all over the Hummer and inside it. Mike continued to talk shit forcing White Boy to shoot him once in the thigh. Mar handed a T-shirt to White Boy and White Boy drenched the shirt in gasoline then set it on fire. White Boy taunted Mike one last time before throwing the shirt at him torching the truck. Big Mike screamed in pain and tried to escape the truck. White Boy emptied his clip into Mike's body.

White Boy and I continued with our plans for tonight while Tone and the others rode to get B. White Boy texted in his phone. Remembering he wanted to talk before I took Simone to the resort crosses my mind.

"What's up man?" I questioned turning down the Yo Gotti CD.

"What up?" he continued to text.

"What have you been into since I left?" My question woke him up from his trance.

"Shit man, you know the night you left from the club those niggas kidnapped B."

"Yeah…!"

"Well soon as I heard that news, I had to put in work to get the ransom money. Tone and Amad helped me rob some niggas at a dice game. After that we robbed some other spots I was watching."

"Oh, so Amad helped y'all do some shit like that?"

"He didn't have a choice after Tone whipped his ass," White Boy laughed.

I laughed out loud imagining the fight. I know Tone fucked him up. "What were they fighting over?"

"Tone figured Amad had to know something about B. Amad told us a story about B and him going their separate ways after hooking up with some girls. Tone lost it and went in his mouth. Y'all niggas think I'm crazy. Yet he is the one forcing Amad to kill somebody."

"Damn shit was going down."

"Hell yeah!" White Boy shouted.

"Well that is good y'all handled Amad's niggas. B is going to kill that man when we find him."

"Trust me Reese, I saw it in Amad's eyes how scared he was when he shot them niggas. He probably left the city by now."

"We'll find him." I pause the conversation to get my thoughts back in order. "Are you over that girl?"

"Reese, I can't get her out of my head. I know her from somewhere." White Boy stared out of the passenger window.

"You'll figure it out." I assured him patting him on the back.

"I hope so," White Boy said in a low tone.

I changed the subject. "What's up with you and Peaches?"

"Reese she is a soldier. I took her to the casino and a nightclub down in Cincinnati where we got into some shit with some niggas. We were kicked out of the club and the niggas tried to get me in the parking lot but she had my back."

"What did she do?"

"Shit what one of us would've done. She pulled out a pistol on the nigga. I have to admit I was slipping. My gun wasn't on me. He could have killed both of us and took all of my winnings."

I put two and two together. All of his damn splurging was from money he had won not the missing money from the safe. Amad had to be the one who stole it. B wanted that nigga but now I do too. We'll end his life.

White Boy and I continued to talk during the drive. We talked about Peaches and everything that happened since I left. White Boy was finally glad to end our ties with Mike and so am I. White Boy's face lightened up when he told me how Big Mike screamed when he was on fire.

We pulled into the drive away and White Boy's phone begins to ring. A huge smile stretched across his face. I'm glad to see him happy.

This game took us through so much that it's good to have someone to make you feel good. Peaches was it for him.

"Bruh, this is Peaches talking some freaky shit."

"Go ahead and tear that shit up boy."

"Best believe that I will." White Boy climbs out the truck.

"Slap that fat ass for me one time," I joked.

"I got you." White Boy snickered and walked inside the house with the money.

I drove away and call Simone to find out which hotel she has for us. To my surprise, Simone is already at the hotel, anticipating my arrival. My conscious began to tell me not to meet Simone and go home to my pregnant fiancée. But the allure Simone had over me is too much to handle and I want some freaky sex myself. Tonight will be the last night I'll fuck her.

CHAPTER 17

WHITE BOY

Peaches allowed me to enter her condo welcoming me with open arms. My eyes almost pop out of my head. Peaches was wearing a lavender satin robe, which reveals cleavage and some of her bra. Hugging her body feels so good. I slid my hands down her waist to grab her ass. She gives me a smile and places her pretty pink lips on mine. When we separated she took me by the hand and we walk to the couch. Her stiletto heels perfectly complimentd her body. My eyes traveled up her legs to her fat ass bubble in the back.

Peaches left me to sit alone on the couch while she cooked. The food smells so good my stomach growls. I took out a half ounce of weed and roll up a blunt. I heard a door from one of the back rooms open up. I nervously looked in that direction and Cherish's thick chocolate ass walks out. She gave me a look of seduction as she clinches onto her towel with water still dripping from her body, "Hi White Boy."

Cherish walked past me into the kitchen. She didn't cover up much of her body. Cherish is a bigger girl but her body is right. She is about 5'7" 160 and have some big ass breast. The tattoo of a snake wrapped around her thighs. I imagined where the snake's slithery tongue was. Her face isn't ugly but is nothing compared to her friends. Shit, if she gives me a chance, I would fuck the shit out of her.

The aroma from the food grows stronger and I can hear Peaches making our plates. Cherish walks back past me into a room with a plate.

"Hey hun are you ready to eat," Peaches approached.

"Hell yeah I'm ready."

Peaches took a seat across from me briefly leaving her legs open just enough to feed my imagination. She reaches over taking the blunt

151

wrap teasing me with her tongue skills. She finished wrapping the blunt placing it down on the coffee table to bring me my hot plate. Peaches made soy glazed salmon, pepper jelly, with sides of boiled rice and asparagus. Then, she brings a tall glass of white wine. I was already high from smoking a blunt on the way over and drinking some vodka, but I'll drink with her just to add to my high.

The dinner was delicious and our conversation is even better. Peaches tells me how an old boyfriend introduced her to her friends a few years back. He taught her how to hustle so she could live her diva lifestyle. The more she talks, the more I notice what we have in common. I did not understand why she or her friends are single. Having a down ass bitch who looks good and can cook, what else can a man ask for?

After smoking two blunts and drinking the whole bottle of wine, we started talking about sex. She climbs on top of me and we share passionate kisses. I'd taunted her with reminding her about the texts she sent me before I rode over. I made her felt like she was telling me some bullshit. She stood up taking my hand and slide it down her panties. The wetness of her pussy got me stupid hard. I'd maneuver my fingers around swirling them around her clit and inside her. The more I move my fingers around the more she gets wet.

"Let's go to my room." Peaches pleaded.

Nodding, I stood up taking her hand. Peaches is walking steps ahead of me and my eyes are glued to her ass. I slap it playfully, watching it jiggle. Peaches turns around to give me a smile showing her pretty white teeth. She pulls aggressively harder on my hand. She quickly closes the door behind us and drops to the floor taking my dick in her mouth. Damn this bitch is a soldier.

Peaches sucked aggressively but suddenly stops.

"Hold on. I have a surprise for you," she says seductively.

"C'mon Peaches, that shit was feeling good. Fuck the surprise we can get into it now."

"Trust me; you'll enjoy this better than just getting your dick sucked."

"Fuck!"

"Relax and get ready for the best pussy you'll ever have." Peaches walked out of the room.

I ripped my clothes off. I laid down on the bed and place my gun on top of the nightstand. I took out the bullets and pour them inside my boots. I folded my clothes neatly in place next to the gun.

Three suitcases sit next to a large dresser. I got up and walked over to the dresser to check myself out in the mirror. A lot of toiletries cover the top of the dresser. I picked up a bottle of massage oil and rub it cross my abs giving them a shine. Curious, I opened her top drawer to see more than a store's inventory of lingerie scattered inside. It seems as if she has more lingerie than the store. I read the measurements of her lingerie. She is a perfect 34-24-38.

I heard someone in the hall way. Shoving the lingerie back inside, I felt something bulky, her gun? Beneath the clothes are all kinds of freaky sex toys. I laughed at the sight but my laughter is soon silent when I pick up a couple of photos hidden under the toys.

I stared at the photos in a state of disbelief and confusion. Both photos are of Peaches, Simone, Cherish, and the girl who has been haunting me. Right then, I knew where I remembered her face. I saw her like a mirage wearing her white lingerie dancing for me at Keith's club, giving me eye contact as she entertained me trying to get every dollar out of my pocket. Like a lightning strike, the image of me shooting her and watching her body tumble down the stairs frightened me. My hands began to shake and my forehead is covered with beads of sweat.

"White Boy are you ready?" Peaches shouted outside of the door.

I broke out of my trance, replace the photos, and close the drawer.

Peaches opened the door and stands in the doorway posing like a supermodel. She took off her robe, revealing her diamond pierced naval. The lace lingerie compliments her measurements perfectly.

She walked pass me and place another bottle of wine down on the other nightstand. Peaches opened one of the suitcases and removes a digital recorder. Amazed, I sat quietly watching her set the camera.

"You want to see your surprise now?" she asked.

"Yes I do."

Peaches dim the lights. A totally naked Cherish walks toward me slowly like she is moving in slow motion. I can't help but smile. I cannot believe that Peaches has set up for me to fuck her and her friend. But even though she seems perfect for me, I'll have to cut her loose after tonight. I don't want her to find out I murdered her friend.

Cherish passed Peaches three wine glasses and climbs on top of me. She softly kisses my chest and caresses my body with her hands. I lye back on the pillows and watch Cherish scroll her tongue down my stomach. She tugs on my boxers. I lift up, and in a hurry she pulls them off. Cherish takes me in her mouth and massages my dick with her soft thick lips. I have to admit she's sucking me better than Peaches earlier. Cherish was able to do multiple things with her tongue at multiple speeds and she's driving me wild.

Peaches stood behind Cherish giving her slaps on her ass. Cherish moans vibrated along my dick. It's an unbelievable feeling. Cherish stopped sucking my dick. She turned to Peaches to slowly take off her lingerie. Cherish licked Peaches nipples and tasted her pussy.

I couldn't take being teased any longer. Getting up from the bed and bending Peaches over putting all of her ass in the air. Cherish laid back on the bed and played with herself as she watches us. I ram myself inside of Peaches' wet pussy and with each stroke I hear her juices smacking. Looking at Cherish in the mirror and blow a kiss at her. Cherish poured herself a glass and downs it before walking up behind me. She planted multiple kisses along my back. I thrust harder and faster. Peaches lets out screams. Her pussy becomes wetter as she clamped down on my dick having an orgasm. I pull out feeling good that she had an orgasm before me.

Cherish pulled me to her and she strokes my dick keeping me firm. I follow her to the bed and she bends over in doggy-style inviting me to do the same to her.

Cherish took every inch of my dick. I forcefully thrust in and out but she doesn't complain. She throws her ass back with the same force. I slow down to prevent myself from having an orgasm but she continues to shove her ass at me. I slap her ass watching her ass bounce back.

Peaches climbed up on the bed and positions herself in front of Cherish with her legs spread wipe apart. Cherish went right to work with her tongue. Peaches worked her hips while grinding her pussy on Cherish face. Cherish stopped throwing her ass at me and focus more on tasting Peaches. I took her by the hips and pound her hard as hell causing us both to orgasm.

I grabbed the bottle of wine and pour myself a glass to quench my thirst. I stood drinking from the glass and watching them touch each other. I felt myself become more intoxicated. I sat down trying to regain myself. I covered my eyes with my hands and before I know it someone is pulling them away and placing them on their breasts. To my surprise it was Peaches pulling away my hands. Peaches straddled me and stroked my shaft instantly getting me hard. She places my hard dick inside her and slowly rides me. I grab hold onto her ass and suck on her breasts making her more moist. Peaches facial expressions do not hide how good I am making her feel. She gently pushed me down to the bed, and continues to work her hips with a good rhythm. She slided up and down my shaft until she orgasms once again. I pick her up and thrust inside her standing up until I cum again.

I laid down between Cherish and Peaches sweating and breathing heavily. Cherish poured me another glass of wine. I downed the glass and hand it back over to Cherish. She placed the glass down and took her turn straddling me. Cherish does not hesitate to get all of me inside her and bounced her ass on my lap. I grabbed her big ass breasts and lick each nipple rapidly. Cherish caused me to have an orgasm in no time. She climbed off and takes my shaft inside of her mouth finishing the job. My toes curled up and I try not to moan myself, but I'm unable to resist. Cherish sucks and licks all over my dick that I plead for her to stop before I have another orgasm. Instead she continues to satisfy me. I closed my eyes tight and feel a sudden movement in the bed. I opened my eyes. Peaches has joined Cherish sharing my dick. I slapped and grab Peaches pretty yellow ass. I felt her tongue and lips get more into it with each slap. I released myself and they continued to lick me until I pleaded for them to stop. They laughed at me but go for each other tasting each other's juices in a sixty-nine position.

After they make each other have an orgasm, they decided to take a shower together. Peaches asks me to join them but I'm honestly worn out. I watch them leave and close my eyes trying to keep my head from spinning.

I'm almost asleep when my cell phone rings. Hesitant to answer, I remain still hoping the caller will stop calling but the phone continues to ring. I look at the name on the caller ID and see its Amad.

"What the fuck do you want nigga!" I answered with an attitude.

"Listen bruh, I know you ain't fucking with me but you need to hear this."

"Nigga I don't need to hear shit you have to say!"

"White Boy don't trust Peaches or her friends. Them bitches are trying to set you up," Amad replies.

"What the fuck are you talking about?"

"Man, that bitch you shot was their friend. All of them work for Big Mike. Peaches is his main bitch. He sent them down here to return the favor for robbing him."

I started to process everything in my mind. I think about our first date. The nigga I fought tried to warn me about her in the restroom.

I ended my call with Amad and quickly get dressed. I pick up my gun and head for the door. I stagger to my feet and slowly open the door. Hearing the shower water running, I carefully creep down the hallway trying to maintain my balance against the wall. When I reached the bathroom door, I recognized Cherish moans inside the shower. I imagined they're at it again. I wanted to catch them off guard and shower their bodies with bullets before they had a chance to do mine.

I took a step inside the bathroom softly pushing the door open. The steam from the shower makes it hard to look inside but I continue to hear Cherish's moans. Without hesitation I take another step inside wanting to get closer before I take aim when a voice speaks behind me.

"Caught you…! You thought you had us."

My mind registered the voice was Peaches. I didn't make another move. I carefully debated on turning around and trying to talk my way out of the situation or shoot. I tried to look over my shoulder but in an instant a loud blast echoes the house. Boom! I fell to the floor by the force of the bullet. Peaches shot me in the shoulder causing blood to flood the floor. Flipping over on my back, I was staring down the barrel of her gun. My gun has slid across the bathroom tile out of my reach. Peaches kicked me hard in the balls.

"Peaches stop fucking around with him and kill his ass!" Cherish walked out the shower.

"This is for my girl muthafucka!" Peaches shouts squeezing the trigger.

CHAPTER 18

REESE

Later that night, I was in the hotel. Simone looked sexy as usual and was wearing her familiar fragrance that smelt wonderful. We sat together on the bed cuddling each other watching a romantic comedy. I couldn't focus on the movie because I kept thinking about Diana. The movie reminded me of our relationship. What am I doing here with Simone?

When the movie ended, Simone whispered sexual comments in my ear. My mind was still tuned into Diana but my dick has a mind of its own. Simone unzipped my pants and scrolled her tongue along my shaft until I was hard.

"I'm going to go inside of the bathroom and put something on for you."

When Simone entered the bathroom she plays some slow R&B music. It's the same song Diana and I constantly played when we made love. I stand and quietly exit the room.

I didn't hesitate hitting the stairs exit to make my fast getaway. I rushed out the lobby doors nonstop heading for my truck. Walking through the parking lot, Simone was constantly calling my phone. I ignored the calls sending her to my voicemail. I speed out of the parking lot never looking back.

Once I was a few blocks from my house I started deleting all of Simone's voicemail and text messages. Before I was done, I received a call from Detective Shaw. He said it's urgent that we meet somewhere where we can talk. Not wanting to drive too far from my neighborhood, I asked him to meet me at a nearby gas station.

Twenty minutes passed and I nervously wait wondering what he could possibly want at this time of night. I didn't feel right meeting him alone but I have to handle business.

Shaw parked his Charger beside me and hurriedly jumps out. His movements make me even more jumpy so I quickly checked my surroundings for a set up. I have my phone ready to record our conversation. I wanted to watch my own ass in case he tried some shit.

Shaw opened the door and sat in the passenger seat. I ask him to lift his shirt checking for any wires. He laughed but I was serious as a heart attack. All Shaw has on him is his standard issued gun.

"Reese this is a nice neighborhood and some ways out of the city. Why did you want to meet this far out…?"

"I'm about to go to the super center and get my girl something," I replied.

"I know how that is. I've been married for eleven years. Shit that is why I work for my local dope boys. The department doesn't pay me enough to keep her satisfied. But I'm not here to talk about our women. I wanted to warn you about a member of your crew."

"Who…?" I asked screwing my face up with anger.

"Some people I work with said Amad asked for their help to rob you all. He told them about your meeting spots, where you all keep the money and even mentioned my name to them. I can't have some young stupid nigga running his mouth about me. If I go down, you go down and a lot of people will be after you all."

I nodded, staring out the windshield. I understood his frustration and I'm glad he came to me with this. Detective Shaw's words boiled my blood. My mind processes thoughts of torture that I have in mind for Amad.

My phone rings breaking my train of thought. Diana is calling me. I know she's wondering when I'm coming home.

"Reese, I'm going to let you go. I know you're a busy man and I have some work to do myself," Shaw opens the door.

I grab Shaw's arm. "Shaw I know this information comes with a price. How about you call me tomorrow? I'll pay you for your time."

"No. This is a free tip. I look at it as a long-term business investment," Shaw closes the door behind him.

I waited for Shaw to leave first. I don't want Shaw to be able to follow me or have an idea in which direction I'm heading. I play things off as if I'm on my phone. I become relieved watching him buckle his seat belt and finally pull off. I watch Shaw's car speed up the street disappearing in the dark night.

When I pulled up in front of my house I see Tone's truck out front and every light in my house is on. Tone must have brought B over so we can celebrate his homecoming.

Opening the door I expected to see my boys happy, but everyone is wearing a sad face. Everyone was here except for Amad and White Boy but I knew where White Boy was. The crew sat in my living room motionless. Ashley and Diana sat huddled together on the steps crying. Diana's eyes caught mine and she rushed over to me with a hug.

"What is wrong with you?" I asked gently pushing her away so I can see her face.

"Baby its White Boy!" her voice trembled.

"White Boy," I said confused. I looked over at B and Tone wondering what he did now.

Diana cried louder and her tears cascaded down faster. Ashley walked over to comfort her.

I stood stunned not knowing what's going on.

"Someone going to tell me something…!"

B rubbed his face trying to wipe away his tears. He looked at me with sad eyes, "Reese come over here man."

I took a seat on the loveseat. I circle the room with my eyes studying everyone's body language. They all remain still except for Mar, who's pacing the floor, pounding his fist against his palm.

Tone sits up looking like some sort of counselor, folding his hands and preparing himself to speak. "Reese, I'm sorry man but the police found White Boy's body shot dead in his car."

"What! My little nigga is dead Tone. Hell no, he ain't dead!" I shout. Tears flow down my face.

"The police found him at the park around the way. Someone shot him up pretty badly and left him inside of his car. I tried to call you but your phone went to voicemail. We all decided to come over here," Tone said sadly.

Knowing Simone was blowing my phone up causing me to miss calls made me feel like shit. I placed my fist against my temple and crazy thoughts race through my mind.

"Reese, I think someone did this to get back at us. They had to catch White Boy slipping because you know he would've taken someone with him," Mar added.

"I just met Detective Shaw at the gas station and he told me that some people he does business with said Amad wants to set us up."

"That bitch ass nigga! I can't wait to get him!" B yells, jumping to his feet enraged.

I stood up, staring B in his eyes, "We're going to get his ass believe that!" I slapped B's hand.

"Why don't y'all take his death as a sign for y'all to stop?" Diana shouts.

"Baby—"

"No Reese, don't baby me. I'm tired of this shit! I can't live like this anymore. I'm going to have your baby soon and every day you are out there in those streets I wonder if you'll come home. This life only leads to prison or death. Can't you see that now? You need to promise me you're done. I don't want to get a call from the police about you," Diana cries.

"You won't get a call."

"You can't promise that. I just want you to stop. Just stop, dammit!"

I stood in silence thinking. Looking at her hurt so bad is tearing me up inside. My street life is ruining the best relationship I'd ever had in my life.

B suggested I stayed home while they tried to locate Amad. I reluctantly agreed. Everyone left the house except for Mar. With a serious look on his face, Mar vowed that he would find Amad for me. His look alone assured me that he'll find Amad soon. I closed the door behind them and walk over to take care of my woman.

CHAPTER 19

REESE

The next day B and I receive a call from Mar saying that he has Amad. Mar and Scotty were in the mall when they saw Amad shopping. They followed his car. When Amad attempted to walk toward some condos they rolled up on him and forced him in the car.

I picked B up and hurry over to Mar's spot. We're anxious to see Amad. B bangs on the door like he is ready to perform a police raid.

"Hold up! Hold up muthafuckas!" Scotty barks.

B and I stood outside of the door waiting for Scotty to unlock all of the dead bolts. When he finally unlocked the door he stepped aside. Scotty has his .357 tucked inside his baggy jeans. His tank top reveals his prison tattoos. I see spots of blood all over his clothing and I knew the blood is Amad's. Mar's Rottweiler barks from the basement. Scotty picks up his bowl of Ramen noodles and eats pointing in the direction of the basement.

Without hesitation B rushed for the stairs and I followed. When we reached the basement, the Rottweiler continued to bark with spit flying out of his mouth. The bloody dog is pulling away from Mar, lunging toward Amad. He's tied to a chair with his mouth covered with duct tape. His body is badly beaten, bitten and scratched. Blood is all over the cement floor.

Scotty walked in. He ordered the dog to calm down and took the chain from Mar. Scotty tugged the chain as he walked upstairs.

B and I stepped around pools of blood to stand in front of Amad. His tired eyes looked as if they're pleading for mercy. B hit him with a right hook to his jaw. Amad yell in pain under the duct tape. I ripped the tape from his mouth. B punched him in his face.

Amad struggled to speak, but before he could say a word, B asked him questions. Amad tried to beat around the bush. B instructed Mar to make him talk. Mar picked up a knife and walked behind Amad forcing him in a headlock. Mar forcefully cuts his cheekbone and didn't not stop until he split his lips open. Amad screamed so loud I covered my ears. Mar laughed but B asked him to stop. B convinced Amad that if he told us the whole story we would let him leave the city. Amad took a deep breath and told us how everything started after White Boy robbed Big Mike. Big Mike said he would be his main distributor if he helped to set us up. Amad admitted he had always been jealous of White Boy's role with the crew and felt as if we were treating him like a flunky.

He wanted to be somebody and getting us out of the way was less competition for him.

B went ballistic. He punched Amad as if they were fighting. I pulled B off of Amad wanting to get more information before we had to kill him. Breathing heavily, B pulled out his pistol. Amad begged for me to stop him. He tried to get us to understand the amounts of pressure he was under. Big Mike introduced him to Simone and her girls to help get us.

My heart felt as if it skipped a beat. B and Mar looked over at me. I can't speak.

I remembered a car similar to Simone's leaving the house. Amad had to give her the missing money. Remembering the many different photo IDs I found in her purse, I realized her and her friends are professional hit women. I felt stupid knowing I could have prevented everything from the start.

I break out my trance. Amad said Shaw had been working for Big Mike for many years. Amad admitted he told Shaw where we were going the night we got pulled over by him and told him where Tone and White Boy would meet his boys at the park. I pulled my gun out and pressed the

165

barrel against his forehead. "You bitch ass nigga! You got my boy killed!" I shout in rage.

Tears dropped down Amad's face, "Reese don't kill me man please."

"You helped them bitches set us up, then you got White Boy killed. Man you really think that I should let you breathe?" I bellowed itching to squeeze the trigger.

"M-man, I was trying to warn White Boy about Peaches setting him up. I didn't know she was going to kill him," Amad stuttered.

"When did you tell him this?" Mar asked.

"Last night when he was at her house, the girl White Boy shot was their friend from Detroit. This shit wasn't supposed to happen!"

"Who is their friend?" B pointed his gun at Amad.

"A stripper who worked at Keith's, they knew y'all were close with Keith so she'd worked her ass to get hired there," Amad answers.

The night I met Simone, she said she had a friend working there. "Where are they now?"

"I guess at their condo. I was going over there before Mar got me," Amad said nervously.

"Damn, if I would have known!" Mar shouted.

"Please Reese don't kill me. I'll leave here today and you would never see me again."

I take a few steps back becoming shoulder to shoulder with B, "No nigga, it is time for you to get what you're bitch ass deserve."

B and I squeezed our triggers emptying every bullet into his body.

I looked at Amad's lifeless body with disgust.

"Mar get rid of this nigga," I said pointing at Amad.

Mar dashed upstairs. Mar and Scotty covered his body with sheets and carried it to Mar's car.

I turned to B. "B, I'm done with the game man. It's my time to escape all of this and put this life behind me. I hope you understand man."

B exhaled, "Yes I do. You'll always be welcome to get money with me my nigga. Take care of your family bruh. I need to quit this shit myself but my money isn't up like yours. This is all I know. Fuck it… I'm done when I'm done."

We left and headed for Simone's condo. I called Christian giving him the 411 about Amad and what he said. Christian isn't surprised. He remembered seeing Amad talk to Simone and her friends at the club. Being cautious about Simone hitting the spot, I told Christian to take the money to the club but first take the dope over to our aunt's house. I ended the call with Christian and call my aunt.

Our Aunt Monica was a ghetto ass aunt. She sold small pounds of weed for her hustle. Her and Keith use to mess around back in the day so she knew what was up when I told her that I needed to use her attic. My aunt told me that I was cool to stash it there for a while but Christian had to break her off some presidents. I ended my call and parked a block away from Simone's condo.

B and I creeped up to their front door. It was already opened. We carefully entered inside searching the rooms with guns pointed it in every direction. Simone and her friends left without a trace of evidence showing that they lived here. B looked at me with disappointment in his eyes. Where could Simone be? Did I miss anything? We rush out of Simone's condo as fast as we came in. I continued to think about Simone and her crew as I drive home.

CHAPTER 20

REESE

Five days after the madness, Christian has invited three popular porn stars to the club for gentleman's night. He had done a great job promoting it. Christian has been getting his hands dirty. I had preached over and over again but he was a grown man.

Tone called me wondering if I was going to join them at the club but I told him that Diana and I had planned to go out to eat and see a movie later on. Tone knew I was finished with the game and only wanted to do business with the club but he admitted that he missed us all together. I got him to understand that I was satisfied spending my time at home with my girl. I was now able to do home improvements and get the nursery room together.

In the middle of the night, my phone rung and woke me up. Christian said he saw Detective Shaw around the club. I was surprised. Would have thought Shaw would be satisfied with whatever money he received from Mike.

B interrupted our conversation. He talked to me as if he wanted to kill a cop. I understood his frustration but I reminded him he was untouchable. He shouted through the phone wondering if I remembered what he had done to us. Thinking about this shit he had done also boiled my blood. I assured B I would handle it.

I walked into the bathroom so I won't disturb Diana with my conversation. I called Keith and told him everything. Keith hadn't known Shaw played both sides. I told him I had some audio recorded on Shaw from one of our meetings. He told me that was smart but if I wasn't in any shit then I didn't need to incriminate myself. Keith assured me he would have Shaw dealt with tonight. I didn't know what that meant but when Keith said he'll do something it will be done.

Not able to sleep, I went downstairs and caught up on some sports news. Sitting comfortably on the couch watching the highlights with my tall glass of juice and remote in the other hand, I was interrupted by yet another phone call. I quickly answered the phone. It had been hard for Diana to sleep now with the baby growing inside her.

"Damn B you are calling early than a muthafucka. I know y'all had a late night," I said answering the phone.

"Fuck all of that. Is your TV on?" B said anxiously.

"Yeah…. Why?"

"Turn to the news!"

Hearing the anxiousness in his voice I quickly turned to my favorite news station. "Breaking News", scrolled across my 55 inch LCD.

"With breaking news today, Dayton Police Detective Earl Shaw has been arrested with approximately four kilos of cocaine inside of his suburban home. Sources say Detective Shaw is allegedly a part of the large distribution of cocaine and heroin entering the city. The detective has been on the force thirteen years and has many grievances against him but his outstanding number of drug busts and accolades outweigh the complaints a department spokesman told us. Sources say that the departments "Drug Taskforce Team" received a tip from the community which helped them make the arrest. Internal Affairs will be doing an ongoing investigation looking over Detective Shaw's career and past arrest," the female reporter stated.

B and I shared each other's excitement and couldn't wait to tell the rest of the crew. I told him Keith made this happen. B suggested we call Keith to thank him. I called Keith on three way.

"Y'all silly…" Keith laughed at our excitement.

"That's what his bitch ass get!" B said excitedly.

"Both of you come by my house later so we can celebrate and talk some more," Keith requested.

"We're on our way," I said ending the call.

I entered the bedroom and Diana is up and getting herself ready to take a shower. By the time I throw on my jogging suit, she was already out trying to decide which dress she wants to wear.

"Who are you trying to look good for?" I asked sarcastically.

"I have to have a reason to look good." She looks at me daring me to answer.

I don't attempted to respond and finish putting on my shoes. I rushed out of the house and picked B up.

B and I are excited, riding with the windows down and enjoying the warm air. The atmosphere around the city changes with the weather, bringing out women with less clothes, kids playing sports, barbeque cooking, dope boys showing their rides, and police posting in every main neighborhood.

We walked inside Keith's house and laughed about what was to come with Shaw when Diana called.

"What's up?" I asked.

Reese you have to hurry home," she whined.

"What's wrong?" I asked with excitement pressing the phone against my ear.

"It's…it's the baby Reese. Since you have left I have been cramping really bed," she stressed.

"Calm down; I'm on my way!" I rush out the door without saying good-bye.

Weaving through the traffic on the interstate my speedometer read ninety miles per hour. My heart pounded harder with each beat. Passing the gas station, I asked God to watch over her begging that He hears me.

I jumped the curb and park on the grass attacking the door. "Diana where are you?"

I heard a muffled scream coming from upstairs.

"Bitch shut the fuck up," a voice I didn't recognize said.

I rushed the stairs taking two at a time barging into the bedroom. I'd become staggered seeing Diana lying on her side tied up with her own scarf. Her mouth is taped and tears roll down her face.

Peaches stood over her with her gun aimed at her stomach. Simone comfortably sat on the edge of the bed with her legs crossed. I remained still knowing my time had come like White Boy's. I just wanted them to spare Diana.

"How are you doing daddy?" Simone asked giggling.

Peaches grabbed a fistful of Diana's curls.

"Ah!" Diana screamed.

"What do y'all want?" I asked cautiously in a low tone.

"You know what we want! We want the money you were going to pay my man!" Peaches shouted.

"That shit is gone. I'm done with the game," I say trying to keep back from crying.

"Now you want sympathy," Peaches teased.

"Reese I know you have some money in here somewhere." Simone gets up from the bed and slapped Diana hard to the face busting her nose.

I hesitated for a moment and give in to their demands.

"The combination to my safe is 23-3-32. I don't have much but you can have it," I told Peaches.

Peaches rushed inside to get everything including our jewelry. Tears flow down my face as I watch Peaches pulled the engagement ring off of Diana's finger.

"Now was that hard baby?" Simone seductively kisses me on the lips. "I see that you really do love her. We could have been something. She'll never be able to complete you. You do know she's the reason why we're here. Your girl wanted to see the competition. She has been calling me for a few days wanting to hook up. I bet I could have gotten her to do anything."

Peaches got on her phone and ordered Cherish to pull up front. "Come on, Simone." She brushed pass me.

"You got what you came here for now you can leave." I notice Diana managing to untie her hands.

"No, I came for you," Simone said shooting me multiple times in the chest.

****

Two days later, I woke up hearing Diana praying. I opened my eyes, and she cries hard.

"Reese I have prayed over and over again for you. Thank you Jesus," Diana cried kissing me.

"Diana what happened to me?" I asked.

"Baby, you are paralyzed from the waist down. The doctors were able to take out four bullets but there is one that is near your spine and they're concerned about taking it out. You might not be able to walk again baby."

I didn't care. I was just happy to see her face and have this all behind me.

* * * *

The doctors entered the room telling me I'll be able to walk soon with extensive rehabilitation. I was not hardened by their words knowing how hard I'll work to keep from being confined to this wheelchair.

"I'll be right by your side to help you walk again. I believe that God has a plan for you and you'll walk again," Diana says sincerely.

Diana pushed me in my wheelchair leaving the hospital. Christian sits in the lobby, talking business with someone on the phone. I wondered where I went wrong with him. All that he had seen he remained lured into the game. He leaned down giving me a hug still on the phone.

I shook my head but he ignored my gesture. I turned to Diana and she knows exactly how I was feeling.

"He has to learn for himself just the way you did," Diana said.

I nodded as she pushed me toward the exit.

I looked up and see the bright red exit sign. The game was behind me now and my new life awaits ahead. Nothing could ever bring me back into the game.

Made in the USA
Middletown, DE
02 March 2020